CW00344313

Lectionary
Advent 2020 to the eve of Advent 2021 (Year B)

Church House Publishing

Published by	Church House Publishing
	Church House
	Great Smith Street
	London SW1P 3AZ

Compilation ©   *The Archbishops' Council 2020*

ISBN   978-0-7151-2371-3 (standard)
978-0-7151-2372-0 (large)

Authorization   The Common Worship Calendar and Lectionaries are authorized pursuant to Canon B 2 of the Canons of the Church of England for use until further resolution of the General Synod of the Church of England.

Copyright and Acknowledgements   The Revised Common Lectionary is copyright © The Consultation on Common Texts: 1992. The Church of England adaptations to the Principal Service Lectionary are copyright © The Archbishops' Council, as are the Second and Third Service Lectionaries, the Weekday Lectionary for Morning and Evening Prayer and the Additional Weekday Lectionary.

The Daily Eucharistic Lectionary derives, with some adaptation, from the Ordo Lectionum Missae of the Roman Catholic Church and is reproduced by permission of The International Commission on English in the Liturgy.

Edited by Peter Moger
Designed by Derek Birdsall & John Morgan/Omnific
Typeset by RefineCatch Ltd, Bungay, Suffolk
Printed in England by Core Publications Ltd

Contents of this booklet

This booklet gives details of the full range of possibilities envisaged in the liturgical calendar and lectionary of Common Worship. Its use as a tool for the preparation of worship will require the making of several choices based first on the general celebration of the Christian year by the Church of England as a whole; second on the customary pattern of calendar in the diocese, parish and place of worship; and third on the pattern of services locally.

The **first column** comprises the Calendar of the Church with the days of the year. Observances that are mandatory are printed either in **bold** type (Sundays), in **bold** type (Principal Feasts and Holy Days) or in roman (Festivals). Optional celebrations (Lesser Festivals) and Commemorations are printed in ordinary roman type and *italic* type respectively.

The **second column** comprises (a) the readings and psalms for the Principal Service on Sundays, Principal Feasts and Holy Days, and Festivals, and (b) Holy Communion readings and psalms for other days of the week. On the Sundays after Trinity, the Old Testament reading and its psalm are divided into two smaller columns, indicating a choice between a 'continuous' reading week by week or a reading 'related' to the Gospel for that day.

The **third column** comprises (a) the Third Service readings and psalms for Sundays, Principal Feasts and Holy Days, and Festivals, and (b) the readings and psalms for weekday Morning Prayer.

The **fourth column** comprises (a) the Second Service readings and psalms for Sundays, Principal Feasts and Holy Days, and Festivals, and (b) the readings and psalms for weekday Evening Prayer.

An **Additional Weekday Lectionary**, intended particularly for use in places of worship that attract occasional rather than daily worshippers, is provided on pages 74–81. It may be used either at Morning or Evening Prayer.

Common of the Saints

General readings and psalms for saints' days can be found on pages 83–87; for some particular celebrations, other readings are suggested there.

Special Occasions

Readings and psalms for special occasions can be found on pages 88–90.

Liturgical colours

Appropriate liturgical colours are suggested in this booklet. They are not mandatory; traditional or local use may be followed.

Colours are indicated by single letters: the first (always upper case) for the season or Festival; and occasionally a second (lower case) for an optional celebration on that day. Thus, for example, *Gr* for the celebration of a Lesser Festival whose liturgical colour is red, in an otherwise 'green' season.

The following abbreviations are used:

G	Green
P or p	Purple or Violet
P(La)	Purple or Lent array
R or r	Red
W or w	White (Gold is indicated where its use would be appropriate)

Notes on the Lectionary

Sundays, Principal Feasts and Holy Days and Festivals

Three sets of psalms and readings are provided for each Sunday, Principal Feast or Holy Day and Festival.

The **Principal Service lectionary** (based on the Revised Common Lectionary) is intended for use at the principal service of the day (whether this service is Holy Communion or some other authorized form). In most Church communities, this is likely to be the mid-morning service, but the minister is free to decide which service time normally constitutes the Principal Service of the day. This lectionary may be used twice if required – for example, at an early celebration of Holy Communion and then again at a later one.

If only **two readings** are used at the Principal Service and that service is Holy Communion, the second reading must always be the Gospel reading. When the Principal Service lectionary is used at a service other than Holy Communion, the Gospel reading need not always be chosen.

The **Second Service lectionary** is intended for a second main service. In many churches, this lectionary may be the appropriate provision for a Sunday afternoon or evening service. A Gospel reading is always provided so that this lectionary can, if necessary, be used where the second main service is a celebration of Holy Communion.

The **Third Service lectionary**, with shorter readings, is intended where a third set of psalms and readings is needed and is most appropriate for use at an office. A Gospel reading is not always provided, so this lectionary is not suitable for use at Holy Communion.

Weekdays

The Common Worship Weekday Lectionary authorized by the General Synod in 2005 comprises a lectionary (with psalms) for Holy Communion, a lectionary for Morning and Evening Prayer, and tables of psalms for Morning and Evening Prayer.

The **Daily Eucharistic Lectionary** (based on the Roman Catholic daily eucharistic lectionary) is a semi-continuous two-year lectionary with a wide use of scripture, though not complete coverage of the Bible. Two readings are provided for each day, the first from either the Old or New Testament, the second always a Gospel. Psalm provision is intended to be a brief response to the first reading. It is for use at Holy Communion normally in places with a daily or near-daily celebration with a regular congregation. It may also be used as an office lectionary.

The **lectionary for Morning and Evening Prayer** always provides two readings for each office, the first from the Old Testament and the second from the New Testament. These are generally in sequence. One of the New Testament readings for any particular day is from the Gospels.

The **psalms for Morning and Evening Prayer** follow a sequential pattern in Ordinary Time (apart from the period from All Saints to the beginning of Advent).

In the periods from All Saints until 18 December, from the Epiphany until the Presentation of Christ in the Temple (Candlemas), from Ash Wednesday until Palm Sunday, and from the Monday after Easter Week until Pentecost, there is a choice of psalms at Morning and Evening Prayer. The psalms printed first reflect the theme of the season. Alternatively, the psalms from the Ordinary Time cycle may be used. The two sets are separated by 'or'.

From 19 December until the Epiphany and from the Monday of Holy Week until the Saturday of Easter Week, only seasonal psalms are provided.

Where more than one psalm is given, one psalm (printed in **bold**) may be used as the sole psalm at that office.

Guidance on how these options for saying the psalms are expressed typographically can be found in the 'Notes on the Lectionary' below.

A further cycle is provided (see table on page 90), which is largely the monthly sequential cycle of psalms given in the *Book of Common Prayer*.

A single psalm for use by those who only say one office each day is provided in Prayer During the Day in *Common Worship: Daily Prayer*.

An **Additional Weekday Lectionary**, intended particularly for use in places of worship that attract occasional rather than daily worshippers, is provided on pages 74–81. It can be used either at Morning or Evening Prayer. Psalmody is not provided and should be taken from provision outlined above.

Using the Lectionary tables

All **Bible references** (except to the Psalms) are to the *New Revised Standard Version* (New York, 1989). Those who use other Bible translations should check the verse numbers against the *NRSV*. Each reference gives book, chapter and verse, in that order.

References to the Psalms are to the Common Worship psalter, published in *Common Worship: Services and Prayers for the Church of England* (2000) and *Common Worship: Daily Prayer* (2005). A table showing the verse number differences between this and the psalter in the *Book of Common Prayer* is provided on the Common Worship website (https://www.churchofengland.org/prayer-and-worship/worship-texts-and-resources/common-worship/daily-prayer/psalter/psalter-verse).

Options in the provision of readings or psalms are presented in the following ways:

¶ square brackets [xx] give either optional additional verses or Psalms, or a shorter alternative;

¶ '*or*' indicates a simple choice between two alternative readings or courses of psalms;

¶ a psalm printed in **bold** may be used as the sole psalm at that office;

¶ on weekdays a psalm printed in parentheses (xx) is omitted if it has been used as the opening canticle at that office;

¶ a psalm marked with an asterisk may be shortened if desired.

Where a reading from the **Apocrypha** is offered, an alternative Old Testament reading is provided.

In the choice of **readings other than the Gospel** reading, the minister should ensure that, in any year, a balance is maintained between readings from the Old and New Testaments and that, where a particular biblical book is appointed to be read over several weeks, the choice ensures that the continuity of one book is not lost.

On the Sundays after Trinity, the Principal Service Lectionary provides **alternative Old Testament readings and psalms**. References in the left-hand column (under the heading 'Continuous') offer a *semi-continuous* reading of Old Testament texts. Such a reading and its complementary psalmody stand independently of the other readings. References in the right-hand column (under the heading 'Related') *relate* the Old Testament reading and the psalm to the Gospel reading. One column should be followed for the whole sequence of Sundays after Trinity.

The Lectionary 2020–2021

The Sunday and festal readings for 29 November 2020 (the First Sunday of Advent) to 27 November 2021 (the eve of Advent Sunday) are from **Year B**, which offers a semi-continuous reading of Mark's Gospel at the Principal Service on Sundays throughout the year.

The weekday readings for Holy Communion are from **Year One** of the Daily Eucharistic Lectionary (DEL).

Office readings are from Table 2 of the Weekday Lectionary at Morning Prayer: Old Testament 2a in Seasonal Time and 2b in Ordinary Time, and New Testament 2, and from Table 1 of the Weekday Lectionary at Evening Prayer.

Notes on the Calendar
29 November 2020 —
27 November 2021

These notes are based on the Rules to Order the Christian Year (*Common Worship: Times and Seasons*, pages 24–30).

Sundays

All Sundays celebrate the paschal mystery of the death and resurrection of the Lord. They also reflect the character of the seasons in which they are set.

Principal Feasts

On these days (printed in **bold**) Holy Communion is celebrated in every cathedral and in at least one church in each benefice or, where benefices are held in plurality, in at least one church in at least one of those benefices, and this celebration, required by Canon B 14, may not be displaced by any other celebration, and may be dispensed with only in accordance with the provision of Canon B 14A.

Except in the case of Christmas Day and Easter Day, the celebration of the Feast *begins with Evening Prayer on the day before the Feast*, and the Collect at that Evening Prayer is that of the Feast. In the case of Christmas Eve and Easter Eve, there is proper liturgical provision (including a Collect) for the whole day.

The Epiphany may, for pastoral reasons, be celebrated on Sunday 3 January.

All Saints' Day may, for pastoral reasons, be celebrated on Sunday 31 October. If so, there may be a supplementary celebration on Monday 1 November.

Other Principal Holy Days

These days (printed in **bold**), and the liturgical provision for them, may not be displaced by any other celebration.

Ash Wednesday (17 February) and **Maundy Thursday** (1 April) are Principal Holy Days. On both these days Holy Communion is celebrated in every cathedral or in at least one church in each benefice or, where benefices are held in plurality, in at least one church in at least one of those benefices, except where there is dispensation under Canon B 14A.

Good Friday (2 April) is a Principal Holy Day.

Eastertide

The paschal character of **the Great Fifty Days of Easter**, from Easter Day (4 April) to Pentecost (23 May), should be celebrated throughout the season, and should not be displaced by other celebrations. No Festival day may be celebrated in Easter Week; and nor may any Festival – except for a Patronal or Dedication Festival – displace the celebration of a Sunday (a memorial of the resurrection) during Eastertide. The paschal character of the season should be retained on those weekdays when saints' days are celebrated.

The three days before Ascension Day (10–12 May) are customarily observed as **Rogation Days**, when prayer is offered for God's blessing on the fruits of the earth and on human labour.

The nine days **after Ascension Day until the eve of Pentecost** (14–22 May) are observed as days of prayer and preparation for the celebration of the outpouring of the Holy Spirit.

Ordinary Time

Ordinary Time comprises two periods in the year: first, the period from the day after the Presentation of Christ in the Temple until the day before Ash Wednesday, and second, that from the day after Pentecost until the day before the First Sunday of Advent.

During Ordinary Time, there is no seasonal emphasis, except that the period between All Saints' Day and the First Sunday of Advent is a time to celebrate and reflect upon the reign of Christ in earth and heaven.

Festivals

These days (printed in roman), and the liturgical provision for them, are not usually displaced. For each day there is full liturgical provision for a Principal, Second and Third Service, and an optional so-called First Evening Prayer on the evening before the Festival where this is required.

Festivals may *not* be celebrated on Sundays in Advent, Lent or Eastertide, the Baptism of Christ, Ascension Day, Trinity Sunday or Christ the King, or weekdays between Palm Sunday and the Second Sunday of Easter.

Otherwise, a Festival falling on a Sunday – namely in 2020–21, John the Evangelist (falling on the First Sunday of Christmas), James the Apostle (falling on the Eighth Sunday after Trinity) and The Blessed Virgin Mary (falling on the Eleventh Sunday after Trinity) – may be kept on that Sunday or transferred to the Monday (or, at the discretion of the minister, to the next suitable weekday).

Certain Festivals (namely, Matthias the Apostle, the Visit of the Blessed Virgin Mary to Elizabeth, Thomas the Apostle, and The Blessed Virgin Mary) have customary alternative dates (see p.8).

The Thursday after Trinity Sunday (3 June) may be observed as the **Day of Thanksgiving for the Institution of Holy Communion** (sometimes known as *Corpus Christi*), and may be kept as a Festival.

Other Celebrations

Mothering Sunday falls on the Fourth Sunday of Lent (14 March). Alternative prayers and readings are provided for the Principal Service. **Bible Sunday** may be celebrated on 24 October, replacing the Last Sunday after Trinity, and appropriate prayers and readings are provided.

Local Celebrations

The celebration of **the patron saint or the title of a church** is kept either as a Festival or as a Principal Feast.

The **Dedication Festival** of a church is the anniversary of the date of its dedication or consecration. This is kept either as a Festival or as a Principal Feast. When kept as Principal Feasts, the Patronal and Dedication Festivals may be transferred to the nearest Sunday, unless that day is already a Principal Feast or one of the following days: the First Sunday of Advent, the Baptism of Christ, the First Sunday of Lent, the Fifth Sunday of Lent, or Palm Sunday. If the actual date is not known, the Dedication Festival may be celebrated on 3 October (replacing the Eighteenth Sunday after Trinity), or on 24 October (replacing the Last Sunday after Trinity), or on a suitable date chosen locally. Readings can be found on page 82.

Harvest Thanksgiving may be celebrated on any Sunday in autumn, replacing the provision for that day, provided it does not displace any Principal Feast or Festival.

Diocesan and other local provision may be made in **the calendar of the saints** to supplement the general calendar, in accordance with Canon B 6, paragraph 5.

Lesser Festivals

Lesser Festivals (printed in ordinary roman type, in black) are observed in a manner appropriate to a particular place. Each is provided with a Collect, which may supersede the Collect of the week. For certain Lesser Festivals a complete set of Eucharistic readings is provided, and for others appropriate readings may be selected from the Common of the Saints (see pages 83–87). These readings may, at the minister's discretion, supersede the Daily Eucharistic Lectionary (DEL). The weekday psalms and readings at Morning and Evening Prayer are not usually superseded by those for Lesser Festivals, but at the minister's discretion psalms and readings provided on these days for use at Holy Communion may be used instead at Morning or Evening Prayer.

The minister may be selective in the Lesser Festivals that are observed and may also keep some, or all of them, as Commemorations, perhaps especially in Advent, Lent and Easter where the character of the season ought to be sustained. If the Day of Thanksgiving for the Institution of Holy Communion (3 June) is not kept as a Festival in 2021, it may be kept as a Lesser Festival.

When a Lesser Festival falls on a Principal Feast or Holy Day, a Festival, a Sunday, or on a weekday between Palm Sunday and the Second Sunday of Easter, its celebration is normally omitted for that year. However, where there is sufficient reason, it may, at the discretion of the minister, be celebrated on the nearest available day.

Commemorations

Commemorations (printed in *italic*) are made by a mention in prayers of intercession. They are not provided with Collect, Psalm and Readings, and do not replace the usual weekday provision at Holy Communion or at Morning and Evening Prayer.

The minister may be selective in the Commemorations that are made.

Only where there is an established celebration in the wider Church or where the day has a special local significance may a Commemoration be observed as a Lesser Festival, with liturgical provision from the Common of the Saints (pages 83–87).

In designating a Commemoration as a Lesser Festival, the minister must remember the need to maintain the spirit of the season, especially of Advent, Lent and Easter.

Days of Discipline and Self-Denial

The weekdays of Lent and every Friday in the year are days of discipline and self-denial, with the exception of Principal Feasts, Festivals outside Lent, and Fridays from Easter Day to Pentecost. The day preceding a Principal Feast may also be appropriately kept as a day of discipline and self-denial in preparation for the Feast.

Ember Days

Ember Days should be kept, under the bishop's directions, in the week before an ordination as days of prayer for those to be ordained deacon or priest.

Ember Days may also be kept even when there is no ordination in the diocese as more general days of prayer for those who serve the Church in its various ministries, both ordained and lay, and for vocations. Traditionally they have been observed on the Wednesday, Friday and Saturday in the week before the Third Sunday of Advent, the Second Sunday of Lent, and the Sundays nearest to 29 June and 29 September.

Notes on Collects

For a table showing where the Collects and Post Communions are published, see page 82.

Where a Collect ends 'through Jesus Christ … now and for ever', the minister may omit the longer (trinitarian) ending and use the shorter ending, 'through Jesus Christ our Lord', to which the people respond, 'Amen'. The longer ending, however, is to be preferred at a service of Holy Communion.

The Collect for each Sunday is used at Evening Prayer on the Saturday preceding, except where that Saturday is a Principal Feast, or a Festival, or the eve of Christmas Day or Easter Day. The Collect for each Sunday is also used on the weekdays following, except where other provision is made.

Abbreviations used in this book

8

Alt	Alternative	P or p	Purple or Violet
Bp	Bishop	P(La)	Purple or Lent Array
BVM	Blessed Virgin Mary	Ps & Pss	Psalmody
DEL	Daily Eucharistic Lectionary	R or r	Red
EP	Evening Prayer	W or w	White (Gold is indicated where
G	Green		its use would be appropriate)

HC	Holy Communion: used where additional references are given to provide alternative texts for use at a celebration of Holy Communion (most often the provision of a psalm or gospel)
MP	Morning Prayer

Alternative dates

The following may be celebrated on the alternative dates indicated:

Chad
– with Cedd on 26 October instead of 2 March

Cuthbert
– on 4 September instead of 20 March

Thomas the Apostle
– on 21 December 2020 instead of 3 July 2021

Matthias the Apostle
– on 24 February instead of 14 May

The Visit of the Blessed Virgin Mary to Elizabeth
– on 2 July instead of 31 May

The Blessed Virgin Mary
– on 8 September instead of 15 August

If any of the four festivals is celebrated on the alternative date these provisions should be used on the principal date:

Holy Communion	Morning Prayer	Evening Prayer
If Thomas the Apostle is celebrated on Monday 21 December 2020 the following provision is used on Saturday 3 July 2021 (G):		
Genesis 27.1–5a, 15–29	Psalms 96, **97**, 100	Psalm **104**
Psalm 135.1–6	Job 42	Judges 18.1–20, 27–end
Matthew 9.14–17	Romans 16.17–end	Luke 19.11–27
If Matthias the Apostle is celebrated on Wednesday 24 February the following provision is used on Friday 14 May (W):		
Acts 18.9–18	Psalms 20, **81** or **88** (95)	Psalms **145** or **102**
Psalm 47.1–6	Deuteronomy 29.2–15	Numbers 20.1–13
John 16.20–23	1 John 1.1 —2.6	Luke 7.11–17
* Exodus 35.30—36.1; Galatians 5.13–end		
If The Visit of the Blessed Virgin Mary to Elizabeth is celebrated on Friday 2 July the following provision is used on Monday 31 May (G):		
Tobit 1.1, 2.1–8 or 1 Peter 1.3–9	Psalms 1, 2, 3	Psalms **4**, 7
Psalm 15 or 111	Job 7	Joshua 7.1–15
Mark 12.1–12	Romans 4.1–12	Luke 10.25–37
If The Blessed Virgin Mary is celebrated on Wednesday 8 September the following provision is used on Sunday 15 August (G):		

Principal Service		3rd Service	2nd Service
11th Sunday after Trinity			
Proper 15			
Continuous:	*Related:*	Psalm 106.1–10	Psalms [92] 100
1 Kings 2.10–12; 3.3–14	Proverbs 9.1–6	Jonah 1 or Ecclesiasticus 3.1–15	Exodus 2.23—3.10
Psalm 111	Psalm 34.9–14	2 Peter 3.14–end	Hebrews 13.1–15
	Ephesians 5.15–20		HC Luke 12.49–56
	John 6.51–58		

For guidance on how the options for saying the psalms are expressed typographically, see page 5.

Sundays (and Principal Feasts, other Principal Holy Days, and Festivals)

Day	Date	Colour	Principal Service	3rd Service	2nd Service
	Sunday / Feast † / Festival ††		Main service of the day: Holy Communion, Morning Prayer, Evening Prayer, or a Service of the Word	Shorter Readings, an Office lectionary probably used at Morning Prayer where Holy Communion is the Principal Service	2nd main service, probably used at Evening Prayer; adaptable for Holy Communion

† Principal Feasts and other Principal Holy Days are printed in roman typeface.
†† Festivals are printed in bold.

Weekdays

Day	Date	Colour	Holy Communion	Morning Prayer	Evening Prayer
	Date		Weekday readings	Psalms and readings for Morning Prayer	Psalms and readings for Evening Prayer

Lesser Festival ‡* [optional]
Commemoration ‡‡ [optional]

‡ Lesser Festivals are printed in roman typeface, in black.
‡‡ Commemorations are printed in *italics*.
* The ascriptions given to holy men and women in the Calendar (such as martyr, teacher of the faith, etc.) have often been abbreviated in this booklet for reasons of space. The particular ascription given is there to be helpful if needing to choose Collects and readings from Common of the Saints; where several ascriptions are used (e.g. bishop and martyr), traditionally the last ascription given is the most important and therefore the guiding one. The full ascriptions may be found in the Calendar, which is printed in *Common Worship: Times and Seasons* (pages 7–22), *Common Worship: Festivals* (pages 5–20) and *Common Worship: Daily Prayer* (pages 5–16). These incorporate minor corrections made since the publication of the Calendar in *Common Worship: Services and Prayers for the Church of England* (pages 5–16).

Advent 1

	Principal Service	3rd Service	2nd Service
Sunday 29 November P **1st Sunday of Advent**	Isaiah 64.1–9 Psalm 80.1–8, 18–20 [or 80.1–8] 1 Corinthians 1.3–9 Mark 13.24–end	Psalm 44 Isaiah 2.1–5 Luke 12.35–48	Psalm 25 [or 25.1–9] Isaiah 1.1–20 Matthew 21.1–13 or: 1st EP of Andrew the Apostle: Psalm 48; Isaiah 49.1–9a; 1 Corinthians 4.9–16
Monday 30 November R *Andrew the Apostle*	Isaiah 52.7–10 Psalm 19.1–6 Romans 10.12–18 Matthew 4.18–22	MP Psalms 47, 147.1–12 Ezekiel 47.1–12 or Ecclesiasticus 14.20–end John 12.20–32	EP Psalms 87, 96 Zechariah 8.20–end John 1.35–42
	Holy Communion	*Morning Prayer*	*Evening Prayer*
Tuesday 1 December P *Charles de Foucauld, hermit, 1916*	Isaiah 11.1–10 Psalm 72.1–4, 18–19 Luke 10.21–24	Psalms **80**, 82 or **5**, 6 (8) Isaiah 43.1–13 Revelation 20	Psalms **74**, 75 or **9**, 10* Isaiah 26.1–13 Matthew 12.22–37
Wednesday 2 December P	Isaiah 25.6–10a Psalm 23 Matthew 15.29–37	Psalms 5, **7** or 119.1–**32** Isaiah 43.14–end Revelation 21.1–8	Psalms 76, **77** or **11**, 12, 13 Isaiah 28.1–13 Matthew 12.38–end
Thursday 3 December P *Francis Xavier, missionary, 1552*	Isaiah 26.1–6 Psalm 118.18–27a Matthew 7.21, 24–27	Psalms **42**, 43 or 14, **15**, 16 Isaiah 44.1–8 Revelation 21.9–21	Psalms **40**, 46 or **18*** Isaiah 28.14–end Matthew 13.1–23
Friday 4 December P *John of Damascus, monk,* *teacher of the faith, c.749* *Nicholas Ferrar, deacon, founder of the* *Little Gidding Community, 1637*	Isaiah 29.17–end Psalm 27.1–4, 16–17 Matthew 9.27–31	Psalms **25**, 26 or 17, **19** Isaiah 44.9–23 Revelation 21.22—22.5	Psalms 16, **17** or **22** Isaiah 29.1–14 Matthew 13.24–43
Saturday 5 December P	Isaiah 30.19–21, 23–26 Psalm 146.4–9 Matthew 9.35—10.1, 6–8	Psalms **9** (10) or 20, 21, **23** Isaiah 44.24—45.13 Revelation 22.6–end	Psalms **27**, 28 or **24**, 25 Isaiah 29.15–end Matthew 13.44–end

		Principal Service	3rd Service	2nd Service
Sunday	**6 December** *P* **2nd Sunday of Advent**	Isaiah 40.1–11 Psalm 85.1–2, 8–13 [or 85.8–end] 2 Peter 3.8–15a Mark 1.1–8	Psalm 80 Baruch 5.1–9 or Zephaniah 3.14–end Luke 1.5–20	Psalm 40 [or 40.12–end] 1 Kings 22.1–28 Romans 15.4–13 HC Matthew 11.2–11
		Holy Communion	**Morning Prayer**	**Evening Prayer**
Monday	**7 December** *Pw* Ambrose, bishop, teacher of the faith, 397 (see p.84)	Isaiah 35 Psalm 85.7–end Luke 5.17–26	Psalm 44 or 27, **30** Isaiah 45.14–end 1 Thessalonians 1	Psalms **144**, 146 or 26, **28**, 29 Isaiah 30.1–18 Matthew 14.1–12
Tuesday	**8 December** *Pw* Conception of the Blessed Virgin Mary (see p.83)	Isaiah 40.1–11 Psalm 96.1, 10–end Matthew 18.12–14	Psalms **56**, 57 or 32, **36** Isaiah 46 1 Thessalonians 2.1–12	Psalms 11, 12, 13 or **33** Isaiah 30.19–end Matthew 14.13–end
Wednesday	**9 December** *P* Ember Day	Isaiah 40.25–end Psalm 103.8–13 Matthew 11.28–end	Psalms **62**, 63 or **34** Isaiah 47 1 Thessalonians 2.13–end	Psalms **10**, 14 or 119.33–56 Isaiah 31 Matthew 15.1–20
Thursday	**10 December** *P*	Isaiah 41.13–20 Psalm 145.1, 8–13 Matthew 11.11–15	Psalms 53, **54**, 60 or **37*** Isaiah 48.1–11 1 Thessalonians 3	Psalm **73** or 39, **40** Isaiah 32 Matthew 15.21–28
Friday	**11 December** *P* Ember Day	Isaiah 48.17–19 Psalm 1 Matthew 11.16–19	Psalms 85, **86** or **31** Isaiah 48.12–end 1 Thessalonians 4.1–12	Psalms 82, **90** or **35** Isaiah 33.1–22 Matthew 15.29–end
Saturday	**12 December** *P* Ember Day	Ecclesiasticus 48.1–4, 9–11 or 2 Kings 2.9–12 Psalm 80.1–4, 18–19 Matthew 17.10–13	Psalm 145 or 41, **42**, 43 Isaiah 49.1–13 1 Thessalonians 4.13–end	Psalms 93, **94** or 45, **46** Isaiah 35 Matthew 16.1–12

	Principal Service	3rd Service	2nd Service
Sunday 13 December *P* **3rd Sunday of Advent**	Isaiah 61.1–4, 8–end / Psalm 126 *or* / Canticle: Magnificat / 1 Thessalonians 5.16–24 / John 1.6–8, 19–28	*Morning Prayer* Psalms 50.1–6, 62 / Isaiah 12 / Luke 1.57–66	*Evening Prayer* Psalm 68.1–19 [*or* 68.1–8] / Malachi 3.1–4; 4 / Philippians 4.4–7 / HC Matthew 14.1–12
Monday 14 December *Pw* John of the Cross, poet, teacher of the faith, 1591 (see p.84)	*Holy Communion* Numbers 24.2–7, 15–17 / Psalm 25.3–8 / Matthew 21.23–27	Psalm 40 *or* 44 / Isaiah 49.14–25 / 1 Thessalonians 5.1–11	Psalms 25, **26** *or* 47, 49 / Isaiah 38.1–8, 21–22 / Matthew 16.13–end
Tuesday 15 December *P*	Zephaniah 3.1–2, 9–13 / Psalm 34.1–6, 21–22 / Matthew 21.28–32	Psalms 70, 74 *or* 48, 52 / Isaiah 50 / 1 Thessalonians 5.12–end	Psalms **50**, 54 *or* **50** / Isaiah 38. 9–20 / Matthew 17.1–13
Wednesday 16 December *P*	Isaiah 45.6b–8, 18, 21b–end / Ps 85.7–end / Luke 7.18b–23	Psalms **75**, 96 *or* **119.57–80** / Isaiah 51.1–8 / 2 Thessalonians 1	Psalms 25, **82** *or* **59**, 60 (67) / Isaiah 39 / Matthew 17.14–21
Thursday 17 December *P* O Sapientia *Eglantyne Jebb, social reformer, founder of 'Save The Children', 1928*	Genesis 49.2, 8–10 / Psalm 72.1–5, 18–19 / Matthew 1.1–17	Psalms **76**, 97 *or* 56, **57** (63*) / Isaiah 51.9–16 / 2 Thessalonians 2	Psalms **44** *or* 61, **62**, 64 / Zephaniah 1.1—2.3 / Matthew 17.22–end
Friday 18 December *P*	Jeremiah 23.5–8 / Psalm 72.1–2, 12–13, 18–end / Matthew 1.18–24	Psalms 77, **98** *or* **51**, 54 / Isaiah 51.17–end / 2 Thessalonians 3	Psalm **49** *or* **38** / Zephaniah 3.1–13 / Matthew 18.1–20
Saturday 19 December *P*	Judges 13.2–7, 24–end / Psalm 71.3–8 / Luke 1.5–25	*From Saturday 19 December until the Epiphany the seasonal psalmody must be used at Morning and Evening Prayer* Psalms 144, **146** / Isaiah 52.1–12 / Jude	Psalms 10, **57** / Zephaniah 3.14–end / Matthew 18.21–end

	Principal Service	3rd Service	2nd Service
Sunday 20 December **4th Sunday of Advent** P	2 Samuel 7.1–11,16 Canticle: Magnificat or Psalm 89.1–4, 19–26 [or 89.1–8] Romans 16.25–end Luke 1.26–38	Psalm 144 Isaiah 7.10–16 Romans 1.1–7	Psalms 113 [131] Zechariah 2.10–end Luke 1.39–55
	Holy Communion	**Morning Prayer**	**Evening Prayer**
Monday 21 December P	Zephaniah 3.14–18 Psalm 33.1–4, 11–12, 20–end Luke 1.39–45	Psalms 121, 122, 123 Isaiah 52.13—end of 53 2 Peter 1.1–15	Psalms 80, 84 Malachi 1.1, 6–end Matthew 19.1–12
Tuesday 22 December P	1 Samuel 1.24–end Psalm 113 Luke 1.46–56	Psalms 124, 125, 126, 127 Isaiah 54 2 Peter 1.16—2.3	Psalms 24, 48 Malachi 2.1–16 Matthew 19.13–15
Wednesday 23 December P	Malachi 3.1–4, 4.5–end Psalm 25.3–9 Luke 1.57–66	Psalms 128, 129, 130, 131 Isaiah 55 2 Peter 2.4–end	Psalm 89.1–37 Malachi 2.17—3.12 Matthew 19.16–end
Thursday 24 December **Christmas Eve** P	2 Samuel 7.1–5, 8–11, 16 Psalm 89.2, 19–27 Acts 13.16–26 Luke 1.67–79	Psalms 45, 113 Isaiah 56.1–8 2 Peter 3	Psalm 85 Zechariah 2 Revelation 1.1–8
	Principal Service	**3rd Service**	**2nd Service**
Friday 25 December **Christmas Day** Gold or W	Any of the following three sets of Principal Service readings may be used on the evening of Christmas Eve and on Christmas Day. Set III should be used at some service during the celebration. Set I Isaiah 9.2–7 Psalm 96 Titus 2.11–14 Luke 2.1–14 [15–20] Set II Isaiah 62.6–end Psalm 97 Titus 3.4–7 Luke 2.[1–7] 8–20 Set III Isaiah 52.7–10 Psalm 98 Hebrews 1.1–4 [5–12] John 1.1–14	MP Psalms 110, 117 Isaiah 62.1–5 Matthew 1.18–end	EP Psalm 8 Isaiah 65.17–25 Philippians 2.5–11 or Luke 2.1–20 if it has not been used at the principal service of the day
Saturday 26 December Stephen, deacon, first martyr R	2 Chronicles 24.20–22 or Acts 7.51–end Psalm 119.161–168 Acts 7.51–end or Galatians 2.16b–20 Matthew 10.17–22	MP Psalms 13, 31.1–8, 150 Jeremiah 26.12–15 Acts 6	EP Psalms 57, 86 Genesis 4.1–10 Matthew 23.34–end

John, Apostle and Evangelist / Christmas 1

If John, Apostle and Evangelist is celebrated on Sunday 27 December:

	Principal Service	3rd Service	2nd Service
Sunday W **27 December** John, Apostle and Evangelist	Exodus 33.7–11a Psalm 117 1 John 1 John 21.19b–end	MP Psalms **21**, 147.13–end Exodus 33.12–end 1 John 2.1–11	EP Psalm **97** Isaiah 6.1–8 1 John 5.1–12
Monday R **28 December** The Holy Innocents	Jeremiah 31.15–17 Psalm 124 1 Corinthians 1.26–29 Matthew 2.13–18	MP Psalms **36**, 146 Baruch 4.21–27 or Genesis 37.13–20 Matthew 18.1–10	EP Psalms 123, **128** Isaiah 49.14–25 Mark 10.13–16
Tuesday Wr **29 December** Thomas Becket, archbishop, martyr, 1170 (see p.83)	**Holy Communion** 1 John 2.3–11 Psalm 96.1–4 Luke 2.22–35	**Morning Prayer** Psalms **19**, 20 Isaiah 57.15–end John 1.1–18	**Evening Prayer** Psalms 131, **132** Jonah 1 Colossians 1.1–14

If John, Apostle and Evangelist is transferred to Tuesday 29 December:

	Principal Service	3rd Service	2nd Service
Sunday W **27 December** 1st Sunday of Christmas	Isaiah 61.10—62.3 Psalm 148 [or 148.7–end] Galatians 4.4–7 Luke 2.15–21	Psalm 105.1–11 Isaiah 63.7–9 Ephesians 3.5–12	Psalm 132 Isaiah 35 Colossians 1.9–20 or Luke 2.41–end
Monday R **28 December** The Holy Innocents	Jeremiah 31.15–17 Psalm 124 1 Corinthians 1.26–29 Matthew 2.13–18	MP Psalms **36**, 146 Baruch 4.21–27 or Genesis 37.13–20 Matthew 18.1–10	EP Psalms 123, **128** Isaiah 49.14–25 Mark 10.13–16
Tuesday W **29 December** John, Apostle and Evangelist	Exodus 33.7–11a Psalm 117 1 John 1 John 21.19b–end	MP Psalms **21**, 147.13–end Exodus 33.12–end 1 John 2.1–11	EP Psalm **97** Isaiah 6.1–8 1 John 5.1–12

Christmas 1

		Holy Communion	Morning Prayer	Evening Prayer
Wednesday 30 December	W	1 John 2.12–17 Psalm 96.7–10 Luke 2.36–40	Psalms 111, 112, **113** Isaiah 59.1–15*a* John 1.19–28	Psalms **65**, 84 Jonah 2 Colossians 1.15–23
Thursday 31 December *John Wyclif, reformer, 1384*	W	1 John 2.18–21 Psalm 96.1, 11–end John 1.1–18	Psalm **102** Isaiah 59.15*b*–end John 1.29–34	Psalms **90**, 148 Jonah 3–4 Colossians 1.24—2.7
			or: 1st EP of the Naming and Circumcision of Jesus:	Psalm 148; Jeremiah 23.1–6; Colossians 2.8–15

		Principal Service	3rd Service	2nd Service
Friday 1 January Naming and Circumcision of Jesus	W	Numbers 6.22–end Psalm 8 Galatians 4.4–7 Luke 2.15–21	*MP* Psalms **103**, 150 Genesis 17.1–13 Romans 2.17–end	*EP* Psalm **115** Deuteronomy 30. [1–10] 11–end Acts 3.1–16

Christmas 2 / Epiphany

If the Epiphany is celebrated on Wednesday 6 January:

		Holy Communion	Morning Prayer	Evening Prayer
Saturday	**2 January** W Basil the Great and Gregory of Nazianzus, bishops, teachers of the faith, 379 and 389 (see p.84) *Seraphim, monk, spiritual guide, 1833* *Vedanayagam Samuel Azariah, bishop, evangelist, 1945*	1 John 2.22–28 Psalm 98.1–4 John 1.19–28	Psalm **18.1–30** Isaiah 60.1–12 John 1.35–42	Psalms 45, **46** Ruth 1 Colossians 2.8–end
		Principal Service	**3rd Service**	**2nd Service**
Sunday	**3 January** W **2nd Sunday of Christmas**	Jeremiah 31.7–14 or Ecclesiasticus 24.1–12 Psalm 147.13–end or *Canticle:* Wisdom 10.15–end Ephesians 1.3–14 John 1.[1–9] 10–18	Psalm 87 Zechariah 8.1–8 Luke 2.41–end	Psalm 135 [or 135.1–14] Isaiah 46.3–end Romans 12.1–8 HC Matthew 2.13–end
		Holy Communion	**Morning Prayer**	**Evening Prayer**
Monday	**4 January** W	1 John 3.7–10 Psalm 98.1, 8–end John 1.35–42	Psalm **89.1–37** Isaiah 61 John 2.1–12	Psalms 85, **87** Ruth 3 Colossians 3.12—4.1
Tuesday	**5 January** W	1 John 3.11–21 Psalm 100 John 1.43–end	Psalms 8, **48** Isaiah 62 John 2.13–end	**1st EP of the Epiphany** Psalms 96, **97** Isaiah 49.1–13 John 4.7–26

		Principal Service	3rd Service	2nd Service
Wednesday 6 January Epiphany	*Gold or* W	Isaiah 60.1–6 Psalm 72. [1–9] 10–15 Ephesians 3.1–12 Matthew 2.1–12	MP Psalms **132**, 113 Jeremiah 31.7–14 John 1.29–34	EP Psalms **98**, 100 Baruch 4.36—end of 5 or Isaiah 60.1–9 John 2.1–11
		Holy Communion	**Morning Prayer**	**Evening Prayer**
Thursday 7 January	W	1 John 3.22—4.6 Psalm 2.7–end Matthew 4.12–17, 23–end	Psalms **99**, 147.1–12 *or* **78.1–39*** Isaiah 63.7–end 1 John 3	Psalm 118 *or* **78.40–end*** Baruch 1.15—2.10 or Jeremiah 23.1–8 Matthew 20.1–16
Friday 8 January	W	1 John 4.7–10 Psalm 72.1–8 Mark 6.34–44	Psalms **46**, 147.13–end *or* **55** Isaiah 64 1 John 4.7–end	Psalm **145** *or* **69** Baruch 2.11–end or Jeremiah 30.1–17 Matthew 20.17–28
Saturday 9 January	W	1 John 4.11–18 Psalm 72.1, 10–13 Mark 6.45–52	Psalms 2, **148** *or* **76**.79 Isaiah 65.1–16 1 John 5.1–12	1st EP of the Baptism of **Christ** Psalm 36 Isaiah 61 Titus 2.11–14; 3.4–7

Epiphany

If the Epiphany is celebrated on Sunday 3 January:

		Holy Communion / Principal Service	Morning Prayer / 3rd Service	Evening Prayer
Saturday 2 January Basil the Great and Gregory of Nazianzus, bishops, teachers of the faith, 379 and 389 (see p.84); Seraphim, monk, spiritual guide, 1833; Vedanayagam Samuel Azariah, bishop, evangelist, 1945	W	1 John 2.22–28 Psalm 98.1–4 John 1.19–28	Psalm 18.1–30 Isaiah 60.1–12 John 1.35–42	**1st EP of the Epiphany** Psalms 96, **97** Isaiah 49.1–13 John 4.7–26
Sunday 3 January Epiphany	Gold or W	*Principal Service* Isaiah 60.1–6 Psalm 72.[1–9] 10–15 Ephesians 3.1–12 Matthew 2.1–12	*3rd Service* MP Psalms **132**, 113 Jeremiah 31.7–14 John 1.29–34	*2nd Service* EP Psalms **98**, 100 Baruch 4.36—end of 5 or Isaiah 60.1–9 John 2.1–11
		Holy Communion	*Morning Prayer*	*Evening Prayer*
Monday 4 January	W	1 John 3.22—4.6 Psalm 2.7–end Matthew 4.12–17, 23–end	Psalm **89**.1–37 or **71** Isaiah 60.13–end John 1.43–end	Psalms 85, **87** or **72**, 75 Ruth 2 Colossians 3.1–11
Tuesday 5 January	W	1 John 4.7–10 Psalm 72.1–8 Mark 6.34–44	Psalms 8, **48** or **73** Isaiah 61 John 2.1–12	Psalms 96, **97** or 74 Ruth 3 Colossians 3.12—4.1
Wednesday 6 January	W	1 John 4.11–18 Psalm 72.1, 10–13 Mark 6.45–52	Psalms **132**, 113 or **77** Isaiah 62 John 2.13–end	Psalms **98**, 100 or **119.81–104** Ruth 4.1–17 Colossians 4.2–end
Thursday 7 January	W	1 John 4.19—5.4 Psalm 72.1, 17–end Luke 4.14–22	Psalms 99, 147.1–12 or **78.1–39*** Isaiah 63.7–end 1 John 3	Psalm 118 or **78.40–end*** Baruch 1.15—2.10 or Jeremiah 23.1–8 Matthew 20.1–16
Friday 8 January	W	1 John 5.5–13 Psalm 147.13–end Luke 5.12–16	Psalms **46**, 147.13–end or **55** Isaiah 64 1 John 4.7–end	Psalms 145 or **69** Baruch 2.11–end or Jeremiah 30.1–17 Matthew 20.17–28
Saturday 9 January	W	1 John 5.14–end Psalm 149.1–5 John 3.22–30	Psalms 2, **148** or 76, 79 Isaiah 65.1–16 1 John 5.1–12	**1st EP of the Baptism of Christ** Psalm 36 Isaiah 61 Titus 2.11 14.2 4.7

Baptism of Christ (Epiphany 1)

		Principal Service	3rd Service	2nd Service
Sunday	**10 January** Baptism of Christ 1st Sunday of Epiphany	Gold or W Genesis 1.1–5 Psalm 29 Acts 19.1–7 Mark 1.4–11	Psalm 89.19–29 1 Samuel 16.1–3,13 John 1.29–34	Psalms 46 [47] Isaiah 42.1–9 Ephesians 2.1–10 HC Matthew 3.13–17
		Holy Communion	**Morning Prayer**	**Evening Prayer**
Monday	**11 January** *Mary Slessor, missionary, 1915* DEL week 1	W Hebrews 1.1–6 Psalm 97.1–2, 6–10; Mark 1.14–20	Psalms **2**, 110 or **80**, 82 Amos 1 1 Corinthians 1.1–17	Psalms 34, 36 or **85**, 86 Genesis 1.1–19 Matthew 21.1–17
Tuesday	**12 January** Aelred, abbot, 1167 (see p.86) *Benedict Biscop, scholar, 689*	W Hebrews 2.5–12 Psalm 8 Mark 1.21–28	Psalms 8, **9** or 87, **89.1–18** Amos 2 1 Corinthians 1.18–end	Psalms 45, 46 or **89.19–end** Genesis 1.20—2.3 Matthew 21.18–32
Wednesday	**13 January** Hilary, bishop, teacher of the faith, 367 (see p.84) *Kentigern (Mungo), missionary bishop, 603* *George Fox, founder of the Society of Friends (Quakers), 1691*	W Hebrews 2.14–end Psalm 105.1–9 Mark 1.29–39	Psalms 19, **20** or 119.**105–128** Amos 3 1 Corinthians 2	Psalms 47, 48 or **91**, 93 Genesis 2.4–end Matthew 21.33–end
Thursday	**14 January**	W Hebrews 3.7–14 Psalm 95.1, 8–end Mark 1.40–end	Psalms 21, 24 or 90, **92** Amos 4 1 Corinthians 3	Psalms 61, 65 or **94** Genesis 3 Matthew 22.1–14
Friday	**15 January**	W Hebrews 4.1–5, 11 Psalm 78.3–8 Mark 2.1–12	Psalms 67, 72 or **88** (95) Amos 5.1–17 1 Corinthians 4	Psalm 68 or **102** Genesis 4.1–16, 25–26 Matthew 22.15–33
Saturday	**16 January**	W Hebrews 4.12–end Psalm 19.7–end Mark 2.13–17	Psalms 29, **33** or 96, **97**, 100 Amos 5.18–end 1 Corinthians 5	Psalms 84, **85** or **104** Genesis 6.1–10 Matthew 22.34–end

		Principal Service / Holy Communion	3rd Service / Morning Prayer	2nd Service / Evening Prayer
Sunday 17 January **2nd Sunday of Epiphany**	W	1 Samuel 3.1–10 [11–20] Psalm 139.1–5, 12–18 [or 139.1–9] Revelation 5.1–10 John 1.43–end	Psalm 145.1–12 Isaiah 62.1–5 1 Corinthians 6.11–end	Psalm 96 Isaiah 60.9–end Hebrews 6.17—7.10 HC Matthew 8.5–13
Monday 18 January **Week of Prayer for Christian Unity: 18–25 January** *Amy Carmichael, spiritual writer, 1951* DEL week 2	W	Hebrews 5.1–10 Psalm 110.1–4 Mark 2.18–22	Psalms 145, **146** or **98**, 99, 101 Amos 6 1 Corinthians 6.1–11	Psalm 71 or **105*** (or 103) Genesis 6.11—7.10 Matthew 24.1–14
Tuesday 19 January *Wulfstan, bishop, 1095 (see p.85)*	W	Hebrews 6.10–end Psalm 111 Mark 2.23–end	Psalms **132**, 147.1–12 or **106*** (or 103) Amos 7 1 Corinthians 6.12–end	Psalm **89.1–37** or **107*** Genesis 7.11–end Matthew 24.15–28
Wednesday 20 January *Richard Rolle, spiritual writer, 1349*	W	Hebrews 7.1–3, 15–17 Psalm 110.1–4 Mark 3.1–6	Psalms 81, 147.13–end or 110, **111**, 112 Amos 8 1 Corinthians 7.1–24	Psalms **97**, 98 or **119.129–152** Genesis 8.1–14 Matthew 24.29–end
Thursday 21 January *Agnes, child martyr, 304 (see p.83)*	Wr	Hebrews 7.25—8.6 Psalm 40.7–10, 17–end Mark 3.7–12	Psalms **76**, 148 or 113, **115** Amos 9 1 Corinthians 7.25–end	Psalms 99, 100, **111** or 114, **116**, 117 Genesis 8.15—9.7 Matthew 25.1–13
Friday 22 January *Vincent of Saragossa, deacon, martyr, 304*	W	Hebrews 8.6–end Psalm 85.7–end Mark 3.13–19	Psalms **27**, 149 or **139** Hosea 1.1—2.1 1 Corinthians 8	Psalm **73** or **130**, 131, 137 Genesis 9.8–19 Matthew 25.14–30
Saturday 23 January	W	Hebrews 9.2–3, 11–14 Psalm 47.1–8 Mark 3.20–21	Psalms **122**, 128, 150 or 120, **121**, 122 Hosea 2.2–17 1 Corinthians 9.1–14	Psalms **61**, 66 or **118** Genesis 11.1–9 Matthew 25.31–end

Epiphany 3

	Principal Service	3rd Service	2nd Service
Sunday W **24 January** **3rd Sunday of Epiphany**	Genesis 14.17–20 Psalm 128 Revelation 19.6–10 John 2.1–11	Psalm 113 Jonah 3.1–5, 10 John 3.16–21	Psalm 33 [or 33.1–12] Jeremiah 3.21—4.2 Titus 2.1–8,11–14 HC Matthew 4.12–23 *or:* 1st EP of the Conversion of Paul: Psalm 149; Isaiah 49.1–13; Acts 22.3–16
Monday W **25 January** Conversion of Paul	Jeremiah 1.4–10 *or* Acts 9.1–22 Psalm 67 Acts 9.1–22 *or* Galatians 1.11–16a Matthew 19.27–end	MP Psalms 66, 147.13–end Ezekiel 3.22–end Philippians 3.1–14	EP Psalm 119.41–56 Ecclesiasticus 39.1–10 *or* Isaiah 56.1–8 Colossians 1.24—2.7
	Holy Communion	**Morning Prayer**	**Evening Prayer**
Tuesday W **26 January** Timothy and Titus, companions of Paul DEL week 3	Hebrews 10.1–10 Psalm 40.1–4, 7–10 Mark 3.31–end *Lesser Festival eucharistic lectionary:* Isaiah 61.1–3a Psalm 100 2 Timothy 2.1–8 *or* Titus 1.1–5 Luke 10.1–9	Psalms 34, 36 *or* 132, 133 Hosea 4.1–16 1 Corinthians 10.1–13	Psalm 145 *or* (134) 135 Genesis 13.2–end Matthew 26.17–35
Wednesday W **27 January**	Hebrews 10.11–18 Psalm 110.1–4 Mark 4.1–20	Psalms 45, 46 *or* 119.153–end Hosea 5.1–7 1 Corinthians 10.14—11.1	Psalms 2 1, 29 *or* 136 Genesis 14 Matthew 26.36–46
Thursday W **28 January** Thomas Aquinas, priest, philosopher, teacher of the faith, 1274 (see p.84)	Hebrews 10.19–25 Psalm 24.1–6 Mark 4. 21–25	Psalms 47, 48 *or* 143, 146 Hosea 5.8—6.6 1 Corinthians 11.2–16	Psalms 24, 33 *or* 138, 140, 141 Genesis 15 Matthew 26.47–56
Friday W **29 January**	Hebrews 10.32–end Psalm 37.3–6, 40–end Mark 4.26–34	Psalms 61, 65 *or* 142, 144 Hosea 6.7—7.2 1 Corinthians 11.17–end	Psalms 67, 77 *or* 145 Genesis 16 Matthew 26.57–end

Epiphany 4 / Presentation

If the Presentation of Christ is celebrated on Tuesday 2 February:

	Holy Communion	Morning Prayer	Evening Prayer
Saturday **30 January** *Wr* Charles, king and martyr, 1649 (see p.83)	Hebrews 11.1–2, 8–19 Canticle: Luke 1.69–73 Mark 4.35–end	Psalm **68** or **147** Hosea 8 1 Corinthians 12.1–11	Psalms **72**, 76 or **148**, 149, 150 Genesis 17.1–22 Matthew 27.1–10
	Principal Service	**3rd Service**	**2nd Service**
Sunday **31 January** *W* **4th Sunday of Epiphany**	Deuteronomy 18.15–20 Psalm 111 Revelation 12.1–5*a* Mark 1.21–28	Psalm 71.1–6, 15–17 Jeremiah 1.4–10 Mark 1.40–end	Psalm 34 [or 34.1–10] 1 Samuel 3.1–20 1 Corinthians 14.12–20 HC Matthew 13.10–17
	Holy Communion	**Morning Prayer**	**Evening Prayer**
Monday **1 February** *W* *Brigid, abbess, c.525* DEL week 4	Hebrews 11.32–end Psalm 31.19–end Mark 5.1–20	Psalms **57**, 96 or 1, 2, 3 Hosea 9 1 Corinthians 12.12–end	**1st EP of the Presentation** Psalm 118 1 Samuel 1.19*b*–end Hebrews 4.11–end
	Principal Service	**3rd Service**	**2nd Service**
Tuesday **2 February** *Gold or W* **Presentation of Christ in the Temple** (Candlemas)	Malachi 3.1–5 Psalm 24.[1–6] 7–end Hebrews 2.14–end Luke 2.22–40	MP Psalms **48**, 146 Exodus 13.1–16 Romans 12.1–5	EP Psalms 122, **132** Haggai 2.1–9 John 2.18–22

Presentation / Epiphany 4

If the Presentation of Christ is transferred to Sunday 31 January:

		Holy Communion	Morning Prayer	Evening Prayer
Saturday	**30 January** Wr Charles, king and martyr, 1649 (see p.83)	Hebrews 11.1–2, 8–19 *Canticle:* Luke 1.69–73 Mark 4.35–end	Psalm **68** or **147** Hosea 8 1 Corinthians 12.1–11	**1st EP of the Presentation** Psalm 118 1 Samuel 1.19b–end Hebrews 4.11–end
		Principal Service	3rd Service	2nd Service
Sunday	**31 January** Gold or W Presentation of Christ in the Temple (Candlemas)	Malachi 3.1–5 Psalm 24.[1–6] 7–end Hebrews 2.14–end Luke 2.22–40	MP Psalms **48**, 146 Exodus 13.1–16 Romans 12.1–5	EP Psalms 122, **132** Haggai 2.1–9 John 2.18–22
		Holy Communion	Morning Prayer	Evening Prayer
Monday	**1 February** G *Brigid, abbess, c.525* Ordinary Time begins today if the Presentation was celebrated on 31 January. The Collect of 5 before Lent is used. DEL week 4	Hebrews 11.32–end Psalm 31.19–end Mark 5.1–20	Psalms **1**, 2, 3 Hosea 9 1 Corinthians 12.12–end	Psalms 4,7 Genesis 18.1–15 Matthew 27.11–26
Tuesday	**2 February** G	Hebrews 12.1–4 Psalm 22.25b–end Mark 5.21–end	Psalms **5**, 6, (8) Hosea 10 1 Corinthians 13	Psalms **9**, 10* Genesis 18.16–end Matthew 27.27–44

Epiphany 4 / Presentation

		Holy Communion	Morning Prayer	Evening Prayer
Wednesday	**3 February** *Gw* Anskar, archbishop, missionary, 865 *(see p.86)* Ordinary Time begins today if the Presentation was celebrated on 2 February. The Collect of 5 before Lent is used. DEL week 4	Hebrews 12.4–7, 11–15 Psalm 103.1–2, 13–18 Mark 6.1–6a	Psalm 119.1-32 Hosea 11.1–11 1 Corinthians 14.1–19	Psalms 11, 12, 13 Genesis 19.1–3, 12–29 Matthew 27.45–56
Thursday	**4 February** *G* *Gilbert, founder of the Gilbertine Order, 1189*	Hebrews 12.18–19, 21–24 Psalm 48.1–3, 8–10 Mark 6.7–13	Psalms 14, 15, 16 Hosea 11.12—end of 12 1 Corinthians 14.20–end	Psalm 18* Genesis 21.1–21 Matthew 27.57–end
Friday	**5 February** *G*	Hebrews 13.1–8 Psalm 27.1–6, 9–12 Mark 6.14–29	Psalms 17, 19 Hosea 13.1–14 1 Corinthians 16.1–9	Psalm 22 Genesis 22.1–19 Matthew 28.1–15
Saturday	**6 February** *G* *Martyrs of Japan, 1597* Accession of Queen Elizabeth II, 1952 *(see p.89)*	Hebrews 13.15–17, 20–21 Psalm 23 Mark 6.30–34	Psalms 20, 21, 23 Hosea 14 1 Corinthians 16.10–end	Psalms 24, 25 Genesis 23 Matthew 28.16–end

2 before Lent

		Principal Service	3rd Service	2nd Service
Sunday 7 February **2nd Sunday before Lent**	G	Proverbs 8.1, 22–31 Psalm 104.26–end Colossians 1.15–20 John 1.1–14	Psalms 29, 67 Deuteronomy 8.1–10 Matthew 6.25–end	Psalm 65 Genesis 2.4b–end Luke 8.22–35
		Holy Communion	**Morning Prayer**	**Evening Prayer**
Monday 8 February DEL week 5	G	Genesis 1.1–19 Psalm 104.1, 2, 6–13, 26 Mark 6.53–end	Psalms 27, **30** Ecclesiastes 7.1–14 John 19.1–16	Psalms 26, **28**, 29 Genesis 29.31—30.24 2 Timothy 4.1–8
Tuesday 9 February	G	Genesis 1.20–2.4a Psalm 8 Mark 7.1–13	Psalms 32, **36** Ecclesiastes 7.15–end John 19.17–30	Psalm **33** Genesis 31.1–24 2 Timothy 4.9–end
Wednesday 10 February *Scholastica, abbess, c.543*	G	Genesis 2.4b–9, 15–17 Psalm 104.11–12, 29–32 Mark 7.14–23	Psalm **34** Ecclesiastes 8 John 19.31–end	Psalm 119.**33–56** Genesis 31.25—32.2 Titus 1
Thursday 11 February	G	Genesis 2.18–end Psalm 128 Mark 7.24–30	Psalm **37*** Ecclesiastes 9 John 20.1–10	Psalms 39, **40** Genesis 32.3–30 Titus 2
Friday 12 February	G	Genesis 3.1–8 Psalm 32.1–8 Mark 7.31–end	Psalm **31** Ecclesiastes 11.1–8 John 20.11–18	Psalm **35** Genesis 33.1–17 Titus 3
Saturday 13 February	G	Genesis 3.9–end Psalm 90.1–12 Mark 8.1–10	Psalms 41, **42**, 43 Ecclesiastes 11.9—end of 12 John 20.19–end	Psalms 45, **46** Genesis 35 Philemon

		Principal Service	3rd Service	2nd Service
Sunday	**14 February** **Sunday next before Lent** G	2 Kings 2.1–12 Psalm 50.1–6 2 Corinthians 4.3–6 Mark 9.2–9	Psalms 27, 150 Exodus 24.12–end 2 Corinthians 3.12–end	Psalms 2 [99] 1 Kings 19.1–16 2 Peter 1.16–end HC Mark 9. [2–8] 9–13
		Holy Communion	*Morning Prayer*	*Evening Prayer*
Monday	**15 February** *Sigfrid, bishop, 1045* *Thomas Bray, priest,* *founder of SPCK and SPG, 1730* *DEL week 6* G	Genesis 4.1–15, 25 Psalm 50.1, 8, 16–end Mark 8.11–13	Psalm **44** Jeremiah 1 John 3.1–21	Psalms **47**, 49 Genesis 37.1–11 Galatians 1
Tuesday	**16 February** G	Genesis 6.5–8; 7.1–5, 10 Psalm 29 Mark 8.14–21	Psalms **48**, 52 Jeremiah 2.1–13 John 3.22–end	Psalm **50** Genesis 37.12–end Galatians 2.1–10
		Principal Service	*3rd Service*	*2nd Service*
Wednesday	**17 February** **Ash Wednesday** *P(La)*	Joel 2.1–2, 12–17 or Isaiah 58.1–12 Psalm 51.1–18 2 Corinthians 5.20b—6.10 Matthew 6.1–6, 16–21 or John 8.1–11	MP Psalm **38** Daniel 9.3–6, 17–19 1 Timothy 6.6–19	EP Psalm **51** or 102 [or 102.1–18] Isaiah 1.10–18 Luke 15.11–end
		Holy Communion	*Morning Prayer*	*Evening Prayer*
Thursday	**18 February** *P(La)*	Deuteronomy 30.15–end Psalm 1 Luke 9.22–25	Psalm **77** or 56, **57** (63*) Jeremiah 2.14–32 John 4.1–26	Psalm **74** or 61, **62**, 64 Genesis 39 Galatians 2.11–end
Friday	**19 February** *P(La)*	Isaiah 58.1–9a Psalm 51.1–5, 17–18 Matthew 9.14–15	Psalms **3**, 7 or **51**, 54 Jeremiah 3.6–22 John 4.27–42	Psalm 31 or **38** Genesis 40 Galatians 3.1–14
Saturday	**20 February** *P(La)*	Isaiah 58.9b–end Psalm 86.1–7 Luke 5.27–32	Psalm **71** or 68 Jeremiah 4.1–18 John 4.43–end	Psalm 73 or 65, **66** Genesis 41.1–24 Galatians 3.15–22

			Principal Service	3rd Service	2nd Service
Sunday	**21 February** **1st Sunday of Lent**	*P(La)*	Genesis 9.8–17 Psalm 25.1–9 1 Peter 3.18–end Mark 1.9–15	Psalm 77 Exodus 34.1–10 Romans 10.8b–13	Psalm 119.17–32 Genesis 2.15–17; 3.1–7 Romans 5.12–19 or Luke 13.31–end
			Holy Communion	**Morning Prayer**	**Evening Prayer**
Monday	**22 February**	*P(La)*	Leviticus 19.1–2, 11–18 Psalm 19.7–end Matthew 25.31–end	Psalms 10, 11 or **71** Jeremiah 4.19–end John 5.1–18	Psalms 12, **13**, 14 or **72**, 75 Genesis 41.25–45 Galatians 3.23—4.7
Tuesday	**23 February** Polycarp, bishop, martyr, c.155 (see p.83)	*P(La)r*	Isaiah 55.10–11 Psalm 34.4–6, 21–22 Matthew 6.7–15	Psalm **44** or **73** Jeremiah 5.1–19 John 5.19–29	Psalms 46, **49** or **74** Genesis 41.46–42.5 Galatians 4.8–20
Wednesday	**24 February** Ember Day	*P(La)*	Jonah 3 Psalm 51.1–5, 17–18 Luke 11.29–32	Psalms **6**, 17 or **77** Jeremiah 5.20–end John 5.30–end	Psalms 9, **28** or 119.**81–104** Genesis 42.6–17 Galatians 4.21—5.1
Thursday	**25 February**	*P(La)*	Esther 14.1–5, 12–14 or Isaiah 55.6–9 Psalm 138 Matthew 7.7–12	Psalms **42**, 43 or **78.1–39* Jeremiah 6.9–21 John 6.1–15	Psalms 137, 138, **142** or **78.40–end*** Genesis 42.18–28 Galatians 5.2–15
Friday	**26 February** Ember Day	*P(La)*	Ezekiel 18.21–28 Psalm 130 Matthew 5.20–26	Psalm **22** or **55** Jeremiah 6.22–end John 6.16–27	Psalms 54, **55** or **69** Genesis 42.29–end Galatians 5.16–end
Saturday	**27 February** George Herbert, priest, poet, 1633 (see p.85) Ember Day	*P(La)w*	Deuteronomy 26.16–end Psalm 119.1–8 Matthew 5.43–end	Psalms 59, **63** or **76**, 79 Jeremiah 7.1–20 John 6.27–40	Psalms **4**, 16 or 81, **84** Genesis 43.1–15 Galatians 6

			Principal Service	3rd Service	2nd Service
Sunday	28 February 2nd Sunday of Lent	P(La)	Genesis 17.1–7, 15–16 Psalm 22.23–end Romans 4.13–end Mark 8.31–end	Psalm 105.1–6, 37–end Isaiah 51.1–11 Galatians 3.1–9, 23–end	Psalm 135 [or 135.1–14] Genesis 12.1–9 Hebrews 11.1–3, 8–16 HC John 8.51–end
			Holy Communion	**Morning Prayer**	**Evening Prayer**
Monday	1 March David, bishop, patron of Wales, c.601 (see p.85)	P(La)w	Daniel 9.4–10 Psalm 79.8–9, 12, 14 Luke 6.36–38	Psalms 26, **32** or **80**, 82 Jeremiah 7.21–end John 6.41–51	Psalms 70, **74** or **85**, 86 Genesis 43.16–end Hebrews 1
Tuesday	2 March Chad, bishop, missionary, 672 (see p.86)	P(La)w	Isaiah 1.10, 16–20 Psalm 50.8, 16–end Matthew 23.1–12	Psalm **50** or 87, **89**.1–18 Jeremiah 8.1–15 John 6.52–59	Psalms **52**, 53, 54 or **89.19–end** Genesis 44.1–17 Hebrews 2.1–9
Wednesday	3 March	P(La)	Jeremiah 18.18–20 Psalm 31.4–5, 14–18 Matthew 20.17–28	Psalm **35** or 11**9.105–128** Jeremiah 8.18—9.11 John 6.60–end	Psalms 3, 51 or **91**, 93 Genesis 44.18–end Hebrews 2.10–end
Thursday	4 March	P(La)	Jeremiah 17.5–10 Psalm 1 Luke 16.19–end	Psalm **34** or 90, **92** Jeremiah 9.12–24 John 7.1–13	Psalm **71** or **94** Genesis 45.1–15 Hebrews 3.1–6
Friday	5 March	P(La)	Genesis 37.3–4, 12–13, 17–28 Psalm 105.16–22 Matthew 21.33–43, 45–46	Psalms 40, **41** or **88** (95) Jeremiah 10.1–16 John 7.14–24	Psalms **6**, 38 or **102** Genesis 45.16–end Hebrews 3.7–end
Saturday	6 March	P(La)	Micah 7.14–15, 18–20 Psalm 103.1–4, 9–12 Luke 15.1–3, 11–end	Psalms 3, **25** or 96, **97**, 100 Jeremiah 10.17–24 John 7.25–36	Psalms **23**, 27 or **104** Genesis 46.1–7, 28–end Hebrews 4.1–13

Lent 3

		Principal Service	3rd Service	2nd Service
				Evening Prayer
Sunday 7 March **3rd Sunday of Lent**	P(La)	Exodus 20.1–17 Psalm 19 [or 19.7–end] 1 Corinthians 1.18–25 John 2.13–22	Psalm 18.1–25 Jeremiah 38 Philippians 1.1–26	Psalms 11, 12 Exodus 5.1—6.1 Philippians 3.4b–14 HC Matthew 10.16–22
		Holy Communion	Morning Prayer	

The following readings may replace those provided for Holy Communion on any day during the Third Week of Lent:
Exodus 17.1–7; Psalm 95.1–2, 6–end; John 4.5–42

		Principal Service	3rd Service	2nd Service
		Holy Communion	Morning Prayer	Evening Prayer
Monday 8 March Edward King, bishop, 1910 (see p.85) Felix, bishop, 647 Geoffrey Studdert Kennedy, priest, poet, 1929	P(La)w	2 Kings 5.1–15 Psalms 42.1–2; 43.1–4 Luke 4.24–30	Psalms 5, 7 or **98**, 99, 101 Jeremiah 11.1–17 John 7.37–52	Psalms 11, **17** or **105*** (or 103) Genesis 47.1–27 Hebrews 4.14–5.10
Tuesday 9 March	P(La)	Song of the Three 2, 11–20 or Daniel 2.20–23 Psalm 25.3–10 Matthew 18.21–end	Psalms 6, **9** or **106*** (or 103) Jeremiah 11.18—12.6 John 7.53—8.11	Psalms 61, 62, **64** or 119.**129–152** Genesis 47.28—end of 48 Hebrews 5.11—6.12
Wednesday 10 March	P(La)	Deuteronomy 4.1, 5–9 Psalm 147.13–end Matthew 5.17–19	Psalm **38** or 110, **111**, 112 Jeremiah 13.1–11 John 8.12–30	Psalms 36, **39** or 119.**129–152** Genesis 49.1–32 Hebrews 6.13–end
Thursday 11 March	P(La)	Jeremiah 7.23–28 Psalm 95.1–2, 6–end Luke 11.14–23	Psalms **56**, 57 or 113, **115** Jeremiah 14 John 8.31–47	Psalms **59**, 60 or 113, **116**, 117 Genesis 49.33—end of 50 Hebrews 7.1–10
Friday 12 March	P(La)	Hosea 14 Psalm 81.6–10, 13, 16 Mark 12.28–34	Psalm 22 or **139** Jeremiah 15.10–end John 8.48–end	Psalm **69** or **130**, 131, 137 Exodus 1.1–14 Hebrews 7.11–end
Saturday 13 March	P(La)	Hosea 5.15—6.6 Psalm 51.1–2, 17–end Luke 18.9–14	Psalm **31** or 120, **121**, 122 Jeremiah 16.10—17.4 John 9.1–17	Psalms **116**, 130 or **118** Exodus 1.22—2.10 Hebrews 8

		Principal Service	3rd Service	2nd Service
Sunday	**14 March** *P(La)* **4th Sunday of Lent**	Numbers 21.4–9 Psalm 107.1–3, 17–22 [or 107.1–9] Ephesians 2.1–10 John 3.14–21	Psalm 27 1 Samuel 16.1–13 John 9.1–25	Psalms 13, 14 Exodus 6.2–13 Romans 5.1–11 HC John 12.1–8

For Mothering Sunday:
Exodus 2.1–10 or 1 Samuel 1.20–end; Psalm 34.11–20 or Psalm 127.1–4;
2 Corinthians 1.3–7 or Colossians 3.12–17; Luke 2.33–35 or John 19.25b–27
If the Principal Service readings have been displaced by Mothering Sunday provisions, they may be used at the Second Service.

The following readings may replace those provided for Holy Communion on any day (except Joseph of Nazareth) during the Fourth Week of Lent:
Micah 7.7–9; Psalm 27.1, 9–10, 16–17; John 9

		Holy Communion	Morning Prayer	Evening Prayer
Monday	**15 March** *P(La)*	Isaiah 65.17–21 Psalm 30.1–5, 8, 11–end John 4.43–end	Psalms 70, **77** or 123, 124, 125, **126** Jeremiah 17.5–18 John 9.18–end	Psalms **25**, 28 or **127**, 128, 129 Exodus 2.11–22 Hebrews 9.1–14
Tuesday	**16 March** *P(La)*	Ezekiel 47.1–9, 12 Psalm 46.1–8 John 5.1–3, 5–16	Psalms 54, **79** or **132**, 133 Jeremiah 18.1–12 John 10.1–10	Psalms 80, 82 or (134) **135** Exodus 2.23–3.20 Hebrews 9.15–end
Wednesday	**17 March** *P(La)w* Patrick, bishop, missionary, patron of Ireland, c.460 (see p.86)	Isaiah 49.8–15 Psalm 145.8–18 John 5.17–30	Psalms 63, **90** or 119.**153–end** Jeremiah 18.13–end John 10.11–21	Psalms 52, **91** or **136** Exodus 4.1–23 Hebrews 10.1–18
Thursday	**18 March** *P(La)* Cyril, bishop, teacher of the faith, 386	Exodus 32.7–14 Psalm 106.19–23 John 5.31–end	Psalms 53, **86** or **143**, 146 Jeremiah 19.1–13 John 10.22–end	Psalms **94** or **138**, 140, 141 Exodus 4.27–6.1 Hebrews 10.19–25 or: 1st EP of Joseph of Nazareth: Psalm 132; Hosea 11.1–9; Luke 2.41–end

		Principal Service	3rd Service	2nd Service
Friday	**19 March** W Joseph of Nazareth	2 Samuel 7.4–16 Psalm 89.26–36 Romans 4.13–18 Matthew 1.18–end	Psalms 25, 147.1–12 Isaiah 11.1–10 Matthew 13.54–end	*EP* Psalms 1, 112 Genesis 50.22–end Matthew 2.13–end

		Holy Communion	Morning Prayer	Evening Prayer
Saturday	**20 March** *P(La)w* Cuthbert, bishop, missionary, 687 (see p.86)	Jeremiah 11.18–20 Psalm 7.1–2, 8–10 John 7.40–52	Psalm **32** or **147** Jeremiah 20.7–end John 11.17–27	Psalms **140**, 141, 142 or **148**, 149, 150 Exodus 7.8–end Hebrews 11.1–16

			Principal Service	3rd Service	2nd Service
Sunday	**21 March** **5th Sunday of Lent** Passiontide begins	P(La)	Jeremiah 31.31–34 Psalm 51.1–13 *or* Psalm 119.9–16 Hebrews 5.5–10 John 12.20–33	Psalm 107.1–22 Exodus 24.3–8 Hebrews 12.18–end	Psalm 34 [or 34.1–10] Exodus 7.8–24 Romans 5.12–end *HC* Luke 22.1–13
			Holy Communion	*Morning Prayer*	*Evening Prayer*

The following readings may replace those provided for Holy Communion on any day during the Fifth Week of Lent (except the Feast of the Annunciation of Our Lord):
2 Kings 4.18–21, 32–37; Psalm 17.1–8, 16; John 11.1–45

Monday	**22 March**	P(La)	Susannah 1–9, 15–17, 19–30, 33–62 [or 41b–62] *or* Joshua 2.1–14 Psalm 23 John 8.1–11	Psalms **73**, 121 *or* 1, 2, 3 Jeremiah 21.1–10 John 11.28–44	Psalms **26**, 27 *or* **4**, 7 Exodus 8.1–19 Hebrews 11.17–31
Tuesday	**23 March**	P(La)	Numbers 21.4–9 Psalm 102.1–3, 16–23 John 8.21–30	Psalms **35**, 123 *or* **5**, 6, (8) Jeremiah 22.1–5, 13–19 John 11.45–end	Psalms **61**, 64 *or* **9**, 10* Exodus 8.20–end Hebrews 11.32—12.2
Wednesday	**24 March** *Walter Hilton, mystic, 1396* *Paul Couturier, priest, ecumenist, 1953* *Oscar Romero, archbishop, martyr, 1980*	P(La)	Daniel 3.14–20, 24–25, 28 *Canticle:* Bless the Lord John 8.31–42	Psalms **55**, 124 *or* **119.1–32** Jeremiah 22.20—23.8 John 12.1–11	**1st EP of the Annunciation** Psalm 85 Wisdom 9.1–12 *or* Genesis 3.8–15 Galatians 4.1–5
Thursday	**25 March** **Annunciation of Our Lord to the Blessed Virgin Mary**	Gold *or* W	Isaiah 7.10–14 Psalm 40.5–11 Hebrews 10.4–10 Luke 1.26–38	*MP* Psalms 111, 113 1 Samuel 2.1–10 Romans 5.12–end	*EP* Psalms 131, 146 Isaiah 52.1–12 Hebrews 2.5–end
			Principal Service	*3rd Service*	*2nd Service*
Friday	**26 March** *Harriet Monsell, founder of the* *Community of St John the Baptist, 1883*	P(La)	Jeremiah 20.10–13 Psalm 18.1–6 John 10.31–end	Psalms **22**, 126 *or* 17, **19** Jeremiah 24 John 12.20–36a	Psalm **31** *or* **22** Exodus 10 Hebrews 13.1–16
			Holy Communion	*Morning Prayer*	*Evening Prayer*
Saturday	**27 March**	P(La)	Ezekiel 37.21–end *Canticle:* Jeremiah 31.10–13 *or* Psalm 121 John 11.45–end	Psalms **23**, 127 *or* 20, 21, **23** Jeremiah 25.1–14 John 12.36b–end	Psalms 128, 129, **130** *or* **24**, 25 Exodus 11 Hebrews 13.17–end

Holy Week

			Principal Service / Holy Communion	3rd Service / Morning Prayer	2nd Service / Evening Prayer
Sunday	**28 March** **Palm Sunday**	R	*Liturgy of the Palms:* Mark 11.1–11 or John 12.12–16 Psalm 118.1–2, 19–end [or 118.19–end] *Liturgy of the Passion:* Isaiah 50.4–9a Psalm 31.9–16 [or 31.9–18] Philippians 2.5–11 Mark 14.1–end of 15 or Mark 15.1–39 [40–end]	Psalms 61, 62 Zechariah 9.9–12 1 Corinthians 2.1–12	Psalm 69.1–20 Isaiah 5.1–7 Mark 12.1–12
				From the Monday of Holy Week until the Saturday of Easter Week the seasonal psalmody must be used.	
Monday	**29 March** Monday of Holy Week	R	Isaiah 42.1–9 Psalm 36.5–11 Hebrews 9.11–15 John 12.1–11	Psalm 41 Lamentations 1.1–12a Luke 22.1–23	Psalm 25 Lamentations 2.8–19 Colossians 1.18–23
Tuesday	**30 March** Tuesday of Holy Week	R	Isaiah 49.1–7 Psalm 71.1–14 [or 71.1–8] 1 Corinthians 1.18–31 John 12.20–36	Psalm 27 Lamentations 3.1–18 Luke 22.[24–38] 39–53	Psalm 55.13–24 Lamentations 3.40–51 Galatians 6.11–end
Wednesday	**31 March** Wednesday of Holy Week	R	Isaiah 50.4–9a Psalm 70 Hebrews 12.1–3 John 13.21–32	Psalm 102 [or 102.1–18] Wisdom 1.16—2.1; 2.12–22 or Jeremiah 11.18–20 Luke 22.54–end	Psalm 88 Isaiah 63.1–9 Revelation 14.18—15.4
Thursday	**1 April** Maundy Thursday	W	Exodus 12.1–4 [5–10]11–14 Psalm 116.1, 10–end [or 116.9–end] 1 Corinthians 11.23–26 John 13.1–17, 31b–35	Psalms 42, 43 Leviticus 16.2–24 Luke 23.1–25	Psalm 39 Exodus 11 Ephesians 2.11–18
Friday	**2 April** Good Friday	Hangings removed; R for the Liturgy	Isaiah 52.13—end of 53 Psalm 22 [or 22.1–11 or 22.1–21] Hebrews 10.16–25 or Hebrews 4.14–16; 5.7–9 John 18.1—end of 19	Psalm 69 Genesis 22.1–18 A part of John 18 and 19 may be read, if not used at the Principal Service or Hebrews 10.1–10	Psalms 130, 143 Lamentations 5.15–end John 19.38–end or Colossians 1.18–23

Easter

		Principal Service	3rd Service	2nd Service
Saturday	**3 April** **Easter Eve** *These readings are for use at services other than the Easter Vigil.*	*Hangings removed* Job 14.1–14 or Lamentations 3.1–9, 19–24 Psalm 31.1–4, 15–16 [or 31.1–5] 1 Peter 4.1–8 Matthew 27.57–end or John 19.38–end	Psalm 142 Hosea 6.1–6 John 2.18–22	Psalm 116 Job 19.21–27 1 John 5.5–12

		Vigil Readings	Complementary Psalmody	
Saturday *or* **Sunday**	**3 April evening** **4 April morning** *Easter Vigil* *The New Testament readings should be preceded by a minimum of three Old Testament readings.* *The Exodus reading should always be used.*	*Gold or* W Genesis 1.1—2.4a Genesis 7.1–5, 11–18; 8.6–18; 9.8–13 Genesis 22.1–18 **Exodus 14.10–end; 15.20–21** Isaiah 55.1–11 Baruch 3.9–15, 32—4.4 or Proverbs 8.1–8, 19–21; 9.4b–6 Ezekiel 36.24–28 Ezekiel 37.1–14 Zephaniah 3.14–end **Romans 6.3–11** **Mark 16.1–8**	Psalm 136.1–9, 23–end Psalm 46 Psalm 16 **Canticle: Exodus 15.1b–13, 17–18** Canticle: Isaiah 12.2–end Psalm 19 Psalms 42, 43 Psalm 143 Psalm 98 **Psalm 114**	

		Principal Service	3rd Service	2nd Service
Sunday	**4 April** **Easter Day**	*Gold or* W Acts 10.34–43 † or Isaiah 25.6–9 Psalm 118.1–2, 14–24 [or 118.14–24] 1 Corinthians 15.1–11 or Acts 10.34–43† John 20.1–18 or Mark 16.1–8 † *The reading from Acts must be used as either the first or second reading.*	MP Psalms 114, 117 Genesis 1.1–5, 26–end 2 Corinthians 5.14—6.2	EP Psalms 105 or 66.1–11 Ezekiel 37.1–14 Luke 24.13–35

Easter Week

		Holy Communion	Morning Prayer	Evening Prayer
Monday	**5 April** W Monday of Easter Week	Acts 2.14, 22–32 Psalm 16.1–2, 6–end Matthew 28.8–15	Psalms 111, 117, 146 Song of Solomon 1.9—2.7 Mark 16.1–8	Psalm 135 Exodus 12.1–14 1 Corinthians 15.1–11
Tuesday	**6 April** W Tuesday of Easter Week	Acts 2.36–41 Psalm 33.4–5, 18–end John 20.11–18	Psalms 112, 147.1–12 Song of Solomon 2.8–end Luke 24.1–12	Psalm 136 Exodus 12.14–36 1 Corinthians 15.12–19
Wednesday	**7 April** W Wednesday of Easter Week	Acts 3.1–10 Psalm 105.1–9 Luke 24.13–35	Psalms 113, 147.13–end Song of Solomon 3 Matthew 28.16–end	Psalm 105 Exodus 12.37–end 1 Corinthians 15.20–28
Thursday	**8 April** W Thursday of Easter Week	Acts 3.11–end Psalm 8 Luke 24.35–48	Psalms 114, 148 Song of Solomon 5.2—6.3 Luke 7.11–17	Psalm 106 Exodus 13.1–16 1 Corinthians 15.29–34
Friday	**9 April** W Friday of Easter Week	Acts 4.1–12 Psalm 118.1–4, 22–26 John 21.1–14	Psalms 115, 149 Song of Solomon 7.10—8.4 Luke 8.41–end	Psalm 107 Exodus 13.17—14.14 1 Corinthians 15.35–50
Saturday	**10 April** W Saturday of Easter Week	Acts 4.13–21 Psalm 118.1–4, 14–21 Mark 16.9–15	Psalms 116, 150 Song of Solomon 8.5–7 John 11.17–44	Psalm 145 Exodus 14.15–end 1 Corinthians 15.51–end

		Principal Service	3rd Service	2nd Service
Sunday	**11 April** **2nd Sunday of Easter**	W	[Exodus 14.10–end; 15.20, 21] Acts 4.32–35 † Psalm 133 1 John 1.1—2.2 John 20.19–end † *The reading from Acts must be used as either the first or second reading.*	Psalm 22.20–end Isaiah 53.6–12 Romans 4.13–25	Psalm 143.1–11 Isaiah 26.1–9, 19 Luke 24.1–12
			Holy Communion	**Morning Prayer**	**Evening Prayer**
Monday	**12 April**	W	Acts 4.23–31 Psalm 2.1–9 John 3.1–8	Psalms 2, **19** or **1**, 2, 3 Deuteronomy 1.3–18 John 20.1–10	Psalm **139** or **4**, 7 Exodus 15.1–21 Colossians 1.1–14
Tuesday	**13 April**	W	Acts 4.32–end Psalm 93 John 3.7–15	Psalms **8**, 20, 21 or **5**, 6, (8) Deuteronomy 1.19–40 John 20.11–18	Psalm **104** or **9**, 10* Exodus 15.22—16.10 Colossians 1.15–end
Wednesday	**14 April**	W	Acts 5.17–26 Psalm 34.1–8 John 3.16–21	Psalms 16, **30** or **119**.**1–32** Deuteronomy 3.18–end John 20.19–end	Psalm **33** or **11**, 12, 13 Exodus 16.11–end Colossians 2.1–15
Thursday	**15 April**	W	Acts 5.27–33 Psalm 34.1, 15–end John 3.31–end	Psalms **28**, 29 or 14, **15**, 16 Deuteronomy 4.1–14 John 21.1–14	Psalms **34** or **18*** Exodus 17 Colossians 2.16—3.11
Friday	**16 April** *Isabella Gilmore, deaconess, 1923*	W	Acts 5.34–42 Psalm 27.1–5, 16–17 John 6.1–15	Psalms 57, **61** or 17, **19** Deuteronomy 4.15–31 John 21.15–19	Psalm **118** or **22** Exodus 18.1–12 Colossians 3.12—4.1
Saturday	**17 April**	W	Acts 6.1–7 Psalm 33.1–5, 18–19 John 6.16–21	Psalms 63, **84** or 20, 21, **23** Deuteronomy 4.32–40 John 21.20–end	Psalm **66** or **24**, 25 Exodus 18.13–end Colossians 4.2–end

		Principal Service	3rd Service	2nd Service
Sunday	**18 April** W **3rd Sunday of Easter**	[Zephaniah 3.14–end] Acts 3.12–19 † Psalm 4 1 John 3.1–7 Luke 24.36b–48 † *The reading from Acts must be used as either the first or second reading.*	Psalm 77.11–20 Isaiah 63.7–15 1 Corinthians 10.1–13	Psalm 142 Deuteronomy 7.7–13 Revelation 2.1–11 HC Luke 16.19–end

		Holy Communion	Morning Prayer	Evening Prayer
Monday	**19 April** Wr Alphege, archbishop, martyr, 1012 (see p.83)	Acts 6.8–15 Psalm 119.17–24 John 6.22–29	Psalms **96**, 97 or 27, **30** Deuteronomy 5.1–22 Ephesians 1.1–14	Psalm 61, 65 or 26, **28**, 29 Exodus 19 Luke 1.1–25
Tuesday	**20 April** W	Acts 7.51—8.1a Psalm 31.1–5, 16 John 6.30–35	Psalms **98**, 99, 100 or 32, **36** Deuteronomy 5.22–end Ephesians 1.15–end	Psalm 71 or 33 Exodus 20.1–21 Luke 1.26–38
Wednesday	**21 April** W Anselm, abbot, archbishop, teacher of the faith, 1109 (see p.84)	Acts 8.1b–8 Psalm 66.1–6 John 6.35–40	Psalm 105 or 34 Deuteronomy 6 Ephesians 2.1–10	Psalms 67, **72** or 1**19.33–56** Exodus 24 Luke 1.39–56
Thursday	**22 April** W	Acts 8.26–end Psalm 66.7–8, 14–end John 6.44–51	Psalm 136 or 37* Deuteronomy 7.1–11 Ephesians 2.11–end	Psalm 73 or 39, **40** Exodus 25.1–22 Luke 1.57–end or: 1st EP of George, martyr, patron of England: Psalms 111, 116; Jeremiah 15.15–21; Hebrews 11.32—12.2

		Principal Service	3rd Service	2nd Service
Friday	**23 April** R George, martyr, patron of England, c.304	1 Maccabees 2.59–64 or Revelation 12.7–12 Psalm 126 2 Timothy 2.3–13 John 15.18–21	MP Psalms 5, 146 Joshua 1.1–9 Ephesians 6.10–20	EP Psalms 3, 11 Isaiah 43.1–7 John 15.1–8

		Holy Communion	Morning Prayer	Evening Prayer
Saturday	**24 April** W *Mellitus, bishop, 624* *Seven Martyrs of the* *Melanesian Brotherhood, 2003*	Acts 9.31–42 Psalm 116.10–15 John 6.60–69	Psalms 108, 110, 111 or 41, **42**, 43 Deuteronomy 8 Ephesians 3.14–end	Psalms 23, **27** or 45, **46** Exodus 29.1–9 Luke 2.21–40

Easter 4

		Principal Service	3rd Service	2nd Service
Sunday 25 April **4th Sunday of Easter**	W	[Genesis 7.1–5, 11–18; 8.6–18; 9.8–13] Acts 4.5–12 † Psalm 23 1 John 3.16–end John 10.11–18 † *The reading from Acts must be used as either the first or second reading.*	Psalm 119.89–96 Nehemiah 7.73b—8.12 Luke 24.25–32	Psalm 81.8–16 Exodus 16.4–15 Revelation 2.12–17 HC John 6.30–40 *or:* 1st EP of Mark the Evangelist; Psalm 19; Isaiah 52.7–10; Mark 1.1–15
Monday 26 April Mark the Evangelist *(transferred from 25 April)*	R	Proverbs 15.28–end *or* Acts 15.35–end Psalm 119.9–16 Ephesians 4.7–16 Mark 13.5–13	MP Psalms 37.23–end, 148 Isaiah 62.6–10 *or* Ecclesiasticus 51.13–end Acts 12.25—13.13	EP Psalm 45 Ezekiel 1.4–14 2 Timothy 4.1–11

		Holy Communion	Morning Prayer	Evening Prayer
Tuesday 27 April *Christina Rossetti, poet, 1894*	W	Acts 11.19–26 Psalm 87 John 10.22–30	Psalm **139**, *or* 48, 52 Deuteronomy 9.23—10.5 Ephesians 4.17–end	Psalms 115, **116** *or* **50** Exodus 32.15–34 Luke 3.1–14
Wednesday 28 April *Peter Chanel, missionary, martyr, 1841*	W	Acts 12.24—13.5 Psalm 67 John 12.44–end	Psalm **135**, *or* 119.**57–80** Deuteronomy 10.12–end Ephesians 5.1–14	Psalms **47**, 48 *or* **59**, 60, (67) Exodus 33 Luke 3.15–22
Thursday 29 April Catherine of Siena, teacher of the faith, 1380 (see p.84)	W	Acts 13.13–25 Psalm 89.1–2, 20–26 John 13.16–20	Psalm **118** *or* 56, **57** (63*) Deuteronomy 11.8–end Ephesians 5.5–end	Psalms 81, **85** *or* 61, **62**, 64 Exodus 34.1–10, 27–end Luke 4.1–13
Friday 30 April *Pandita Mary Ramabai, translator, 1922*	W	Acts 13.26–33 Psalm 2 John 14.1–6	Psalm 33 *or* **51**, 54 Deuteronomy 12.1–14 Ephesians 6.1–9	Psalms **36**, 40 *or* **38** Exodus 35.20—36.7 Luke 4.14–30 *or:* 1st EP of Philip and James, Apostles: Psalm 25; Isaiah 40.27–end; John 12.20–26

		Principal Service	3rd Service	2nd Service
Saturday 1 May Philip and James, Apostles	R	Isaiah 30.15–21 Psalm 119.1–8 Ephesians 1.3–10 John 14.1–14	MP Psalms 139, 146 Proverbs 4.10–18 James 1.1–12	EP Psalm 149 Job 23.1–12 John 1.43–end

		Principal Service	3rd Service	2nd Service
Sunday 2 May **5th Sunday of Easter**	W	[Baruch 3.9–15, 32—4.4 or Genesis 22.1–18] Acts 8.26–end † Psalm 22.25–end 1 John 4.7–end John 15.1–8 *† The reading from Acts must be used as either the first or second reading.*	Psalm 44.16–end 2 Maccabees 7.7–14 or Daniel 3.16–28 Hebrews 11.32—12.2	Psalm 96 Isaiah 60.1–14 Revelation 3.1–13 HC Mark 16.9–16
		Holy Communion	**Morning Prayer**	
Monday 3 May	W	Acts 14.5–18 Psalm 118.1–3, 14–15 John 14.21–26	Psalm **145** or **71** Deuteronomy 16.1–20 1 Peter 1.1–12	Psalm **105** or **72, 75** Numbers 9.15–end; 10.33–end Luke 4.38–end
Tuesday 4 May English saints and martyrs of the Reformation Era	W	Acts 14.19–end Psalm 145.10–end John 14.27–end *Lesser Festival eucharistic lectionary:* Isaiah 43.1–7 or Ecclesiasticus 2.10–17 Psalm 87 2 Corinthians 4.5–12 John 12.20–26	Psalms **19,** 147.1–12 or **73** Deuteronomy 17.8–end 1 Peter 1.13–end	Psalms 96, **97** or **74** Numbers 11.1–33 Luke 5.1–11
Wednesday 5 May	W	Acts 15.1–6 Psalm 122.1–5 John 15.1–8	Psalms **30,** 147.13–end or **77** Deuteronomy 18.9–end 1 Peter 2.1–10	Psalms 98, **99,** 100 or **119.81–104** Numbers 12 Luke 5.12–26
Thursday 6 May	W	Acts 15.7–21 Psalm 96.1–3, 7–10 John 15.9–11	Psalms **57,** 148 or **78.1–39*** Deuteronomy 19 1 Peter 2.11–end	Psalm **104** or **78.40–end*** Numbers 13.1–3, 17–end Luke 5.27–end
Friday 7 May	W	Acts 15.22–31 Psalm 57.8–end John 15.12–17	Psalms **138,** 149 or **55** Deuteronomy 21.22—22.8 1 Peter 3.1–12	Psalm 66 or **69** Numbers 14.1–25 Luke 6.1–11
Saturday 8 May Julian of Norwich, spiritual writer, c.1417 (see p.86)	W	Acts 16.1–10 Psalm 100 John 15.18–21	Psalms **146,** 150 or **76,** 79 Deuteronomy 24.5–end 1 Peter 3.13–end	Psalm **118** or 81, **84** Numbers 14.26–end Luke 6.12–26

			Principal Service	3rd Service	2nd Service
Sunday	**9 May** **6th Sunday of Easter**	W	[Isaiah 55.1–11] Acts 10.44-end † Psalm 98 1 John 5.1–6 John 15.9–17 † *The reading from Acts must be used as either the first or second reading.*	Psalm 104.26–32 Ezekiel 47.1–12 John 2.1–19	Psalm 45 Song of Solomon 4.16—5.2; 8.6,7 Revelation 3.14-end HC Luke 22.24–30

			Holy Communion	Morning Prayer	Evening Prayer
Monday	**10 May** Rogation Day	W	Acts 16.11–15 Psalm 149.1–5 John 15.26—16.4	Psalms 65, 67 or 80, 82 Deuteronomy 26 1 Peter 4.1–11	Psalms 121, 122, 123 or **85**, 86 Numbers 16.1–35 Luke 6.27–38
Tuesday	**11 May** Rogation Day	W	Acts 16.22–34 Psalm 138 John 16.5–11	Psalms 124, 125, **126**, 127 or 87, **89.1–18** Deuteronomy 28.1–14 1 Peter 4.12-end	Psalms **128**, 129, 130, 131 or **89.19-end** Numbers 16.36-end Luke 6.39-end
Wednesday	**12 May** Rogation Day *Gregory Dix, priest, monk, scholar, 1952*	W	Acts 17.15, 22—18.1 Psalm 148.1–2, 11-end John 16.12–15	Psalms **132**, 133 or **119.105–128** Deuteronomy 28.58-end 1 Peter 5	**1st EP of Ascension Day** Psalms 15, 24 2 Samuel 23.1–5 Colossians 2.20—3.4

			Principal Service	3rd Service	2nd Service
Thursday	**13 May** **Ascension Day**	Gold or W	Acts 1.1–11 † or Daniel 7.9–14 Psalm 47 or Psalm 93 Ephesians 1.15-end or Acts 1.1–11 † Luke 24.44-end † *The reading from Acts must be used as either the first or second reading.*	MP Psalms 110, 150 Isaiah 52.7-end Hebrews 7.[11–25] 26-end	EP Psalm 8 Song of the Three 29–37 or 2 Kings 2.1–15 Revelation 5 HC Matthew 28.16-end

The nine days after Ascension Day until the eve of Pentecost are observed as days of prayer and preparation for the celebration of the outpouring of the Holy Spirit.

From 15–22 May, in preparation for the Day of Pentecost, an alternative sequence of daily readings for use at the one of the offices is marked with an asterisk *.

			Holy Communion	Morning Prayer	Evening Prayer
Friday	**14 May** Matthias the Apostle	R	Isaiah 22.15-end or Acts 1.15–end Psalm 15 Acts 1.15–end or 1 Corinthians 4.1–7 John 15.9–17	MP Psalms 16, 147.1–12 1 Samuel 2.27–35 Acts 2.37–end	EP Psalm 80 1 Samuel 16.1–13a Matthew 7.15–27
Saturday	**15 May**	W	Acts 18.22-end Psalm 47.1–2, 7-end John 16.23–28	Psalms 21, 47 or 96, **97**, 100 Deuteronomy 30 1 John 2.7–17 *Numbers 11.16–17, 24–29; 1 Corinthians 2	Psalms 84, **85** or **104** Numbers 21.4–9 Luke 7.18–35

Easter 7

		Principal Service	3rd Service	2nd Service
Sunday	16 May W **7th Sunday of Easter** *Sunday after Ascension Day*	[Ezekiel 36.24–28] Acts 1.15–17, 21–end † Psalm 1 1 John 5.9–13 John 17.6–19 † *The reading from Acts must be used as either the first or second reading.*	Psalm 76 Isaiah 14.3–15 Revelation 14.1–13	Psalm 147.1–12 Isaiah 61 Luke 4.14–21
		Holy Communion	**Morning Prayer**	**Evening Prayer**
Monday	17 May W	Acts 19.1–8 Psalm 68.1–6 John 16.29–end	Psalms 93, 96, 97 or **98**, 99, 101 Deuteronomy 31.1–13 1 John 2.18–end *Numbers 27.15–end; 1 Corinthians 3*	Psalm **18** or **105*** (or 103) Numbers 22.1–35 Luke 7.36–end
Tuesday	18 May W	Acts 20.17–27 Psalm 68.9–10, 18–19 John 17.1–11	Psalms 98, **99**, 100 or **106*** (or 103) Deuteronomy 31.14–29 1 John 3.1–10 *1 Samuel 10.1–10; 1 Corinthians 12.1–13*	Psalm **68** or **107*** Numbers 22.36—23.12 Luke 8.1–15
Wednesday	19 May W Dunstan, archbishop, monastic reformer, 988 (see p.85)	Acts 20.28–end Psalm 68.27–28, 32–end John 17.11–19	Psalms 2, **29** or 110, **111**, 112 Deuteronomy 31.30—32.14 1 John 3.11–end *1 Kings 19.1–18; Matthew 3.13–end*	Psalms 36, **46** or **119.129–152** Numbers 23.13–end Luke 8.16–25
Thursday	20 May W Alcuin, deacon, abbot, 804 (see p.86)	Acts 22.30; 23.6–11 Psalm 16.1, 5–end John 17.20–end	Psalms **24**, 72 or 113, **115** Deuteronomy 32.15–47 1 John 4.1–6 *Ezekiel 11.14–20; Matthew 9.35—10.20*	Psalm 139 or 114, **116**, 117 Numbers 24 Luke 8.26–39
Friday	21 May W *Helena, protector of the Holy Places*, 330	Acts 25.13–21 Psalm 103.1–2, 11–12, 19–20 John 21.15–19	Psalms **28**, 30 or **139** Deuteronomy 33 1 John 4.7–end *Ezekiel 36.22–28; Matthew 12.22–32*	Psalm **147** or **130**, 131, 137 Numbers 27.12–end Luke 8.40–end
Saturday	22 May W	Acts 28.16–20, 30–end Psalm 11.4–end John 21.20–end	Psalms 42, **43** or 120, **121**, 122 Deuteronomy 32.48–end, 34 1 John 5 *Micah 3.1–8; Ephesians 6.10–20 (at MP only)*	**1st EP of Pentecost** Psalm 48 Deuteronomy 16.9–15 John 7.37–39

Pentecost / Ordinary Time

	Principal Service	3rd Service	2nd Service
	Holy Communion	**Morning Prayer**	**Evening Prayer**
Sunday **23 May** **Pentecost** *Whit Sunday* R	Acts 2.1–21 † or Ezekiel 37.1–14 Psalm 104.26–36, 37b [or 104.26–end] Romans 8.22–27 or Acts 2.1–21 † John 15.26–27; 16.4b–15 † The reading from Acts must be used as either the first or second reading.	MP Psalm 145 Isaiah 11.1–9 or Wisdom 7.15–23 [24–27] 1 Corinthians 12.4–13	EP Psalm 139.1–11 [13–18, 23–24] Ezekiel 36.22–28 Acts 2.22–38 HC John 20.19–23
Monday **24 May** *Gw* John and Charles Wesley, evangelists, hymn writers, 1791 and 1788 (see p.85) Ordinary Time resumes today DEL week 8	Ecclesiasticus 17.24–29 or James 3.13–end Psalm 32.1–8 or 19.7–end Mark 10.17–27	Psalms 123, 124, 125, 126 Job 1 Romans 1.1–17	Psalms 127, 128, 129 Joshua 1 Luke 9.18–27
Tuesday **25 May** *Gw* The Venerable Bede, monk, scholar, historian, 735 (see p.86) Aldhelm, bishop, 709	Ecclesiasticus 35.1–12 or James 4.1–10 Psalm 50.1–6 or 55.7–9, 24 Mark 10.28–31	Psalms 132, 133 Job 2 Romans 1.18–end	Psalms (134) 135 Joshua 2 Luke 9.28–36
Wednesday **26 May** *Gw* Augustine, archbishop, 605 (see p.85) *John Calvin, reformer, 1564* *Philip Neri, founder of the Oratorians, spiritual guide, 1595*	Ecclesiasticus 36.1–2, 4–5, 10–17 or James 4.13–end Psalm 79.8–9, 12, 14 or 49.1–2, 5–10 Mark 10.32–45	Psalm 119.153–end Job 3 Romans 2.1–16	Psalm 136 Joshua 3 Luke 9.37–50
Thursday **27 May** G	Ecclesiasticus 42.15–end or James 5.1–6 Psalm 33.1–9 or 49.12–20 Mark 10.46–end	Psalms 143, 146 Job 4 Romans 2.17–end	Psalms 138, 140, 141 Joshua 4.1–5.1 Luke 9.51–end
Friday **28 May** *G* *Lanfranc, monk, archbishop, scholar, 1089*	Ecclesiasticus 44.1, 9–13 or James 5.9–12 Psalm 149.1–5 or 103.1–4, 8–13 Mark 11.11–26	Psalms 142, 144 Job 5 Romans 3.1–20	Psalm 145 Joshua 5.2–end Luke 10.1–16
Saturday **29 May** G	Ecclesiasticus 51.12b–20a or James 5.13–end Psalm 19.7–end or 141.1–4 Mark 11.27–end	Psalm 147 Job 6 Romans 3.21–end	**1st EP of Trinity Sunday** Psalms 97, 98 Isaiah 40.12–end Mark 1.1–13

Trinity Sunday

If Corpus Christi is kept as a Festival:

			Principal Service	3rd Service	2nd Service
Sunday	**30 May** Trinity Sunday	*Gold or W*	Isaiah 6.1–8 Psalm 29 Romans 8.12–17 John 3.1–17	MP Psalm 33.1–12 Proverbs 8.1–4, 22–31 2 Corinthians 13.[5–10] 11–end	EP Psalm 104.1–10 Ezekiel 1.4–10, 22–28a Revelation 4 HC Mark 1.1–13
Monday	**31 May** Visit of the Blessed Virgin Mary to Elizabeth	*W*	Zephaniah 3.14–18 Psalm 113 Romans 12.9–16 Luke 1.39–49 [50–56]	MP Psalms 85, 150 1 Samuel 2.1–10 Mark 3.31–end	EP Psalms 122, 127, 128 Zechariah 2.10–end John 3.25–30

			Holy Communion	Morning Prayer	Evening Prayer
Tuesday	**1 June** Justin, martyr, c.165 (see p.83) DEL week 9	*Gr*	Tobit 2.9–end or 1 Peter 1.10–16 Psalm 112 or 98.1–5 Mark 12.13–17	Psalms 5, 6, (8) Job 8 Romans 4.13–end	Psalms 9, 10* Joshua 7.16–end Luke 10.38–end
Wednesday	**2 June**	*G*	Tobit 3.1–11, 16–end or 1 Peter 1.18–end Psalm 25.1–8 or 147.13–end Mark 12.18–27	Psalm 119.1–32 Job 9 Romans 5.1–11	Psalms 11, 12, 13 Joshua 8.1–29 Luke 11.1–13 *or: 1st EP of Corpus Christi:* Psalms 110, 111; Exodus 16.2–15; John 6.22–35

Alternatively Corpus Christi may be kept as a Lesser Festival, and either these readings or those given for 3 June on page 43 may be used.

			Principal Service	3rd Service	2nd Service
Thursday	**3 June** Day of Thanksgiving for the Institution of Holy Communion (Corpus Christi)	*W*	Genesis 14.18–20 Psalm 116.10–end 1 Corinthians 11.23–26 John 6.51–58	MP Psalm 147 Deuteronomy 8.2–16 1 Corinthians 10.1–17	EP Psalms 23, 42, 43 Proverbs 9.1–5 Luke 9.11–17

			Holy Communion	Morning Prayer	Evening Prayer
Friday	**4 June** Petroc, abbot, 6th cent.	*G*	Tobit 11.5–15 or 1 Peter 4.7–13 Psalm 146 or 96.10–end Mark 12.35–37	Psalms 17, 19 Job 11 Romans 6.1–14	Psalm 22 Joshua 9.3–26 Luke 11.29–36
Saturday	**5 June** Boniface (Wynfrith), bishop, martyr, 754 (see p.83)	*Gr*	Tobit 12.1, 5–15, 20a or Jude 17, 20–end Psalm 103.1, 8–13 or 63.1–6 Mark 12.38–end	Psalms 20, 21, 23 Job 12 Romans 6.15–end	Psalms 24, 25 Joshua 10.1–15 Luke 11.37–end

Trinity Sunday

If Corpus Christi is not kept as a Festival:

		Holy Communion	Morning Prayer	Evening Prayer
Sunday	**30 May** Trinity Sunday	Gold or W	Isaiah 6.1–8 Psalm 29 Romans 8.12–17 John 3.1–17	MP Psalm 33.1–12 Proverbs 8.1–4, 22–31 2 Corinthians 13.[5–10] 11–end	EP Psalm 104.1–10 Ezekiel 1.4–10, 22–28a Revelation 4 HC Mark 1.1–13
Monday	**31 May** Visit of the Blessed Virgin Mary to Elizabeth	W	Zephaniah 3.14–18 Psalm 113 Romans 12.9–16 Luke 1.39–49 [50–56]	MP Psalms 85, 150 1 Samuel 2.1–10 Mark 3.31–end	EP Psalms 122, 127, 128 Zechariah 2.10–end John 3.25–30
Tuesday	**1 June** Justin, martyr, c.165 (see p.83) DEL week 9	Gr	Tobit 2.9–end or 1 Peter 1.10–16 Psalm 112 or 98.1–5 Mark 12.13–17	Psalms 5, 6, (8) Job 8 Romans 4.13–end	Psalm **9**, 10* Joshua 7.16–end Luke 10.38–end
Wednesday	**2 June**	G	Tobit 3.1–11, 16–end or 1 Peter 1.18–end Psalm 25.1–8 or 147.13–end Mark 12.18–27	Psalm 1**19**.**1–32** Job 9 Romans 5.1–11	Psalms 1**1**, 12, 13 Joshua 8.1–29 Luke 11.1–13
Thursday	**3 June** Day of Thanksgiving for the Institution of Holy Communion (Corpus Christi) *Martyrs of Uganda, 1885–7, 1977*	Gw	Tobit 6.10–11, 7.1–15, 8.4–8 or 1 Peter 2.2–5, 9–12 Psalm 128 or 100 Mark 12.28–34	Psalms 14, **15**, 16 Job 10 Romans 5.12–end	Psalm 1**8*** Joshua 8.30–end Luke 11.14–28
	If Corpus Christi is kept as a Lesser Festival, either these readings or those given for 3 June on page 42 may be used.				
Friday	**4 June** *Petroc, abbot, 6th cent.*	G	Tobit 11.5–15 or 1 Peter 4.7–13 Psalm 146 or 96.10–end Mark 12.35–37	Psalms 17, **19** Job 11 Romans 6.1–14	Psalm **22** Joshua 9.3–26 Luke 11.29–36
Saturday	**5 June** Boniface (Wynfrith), bishop, martyr, 754 (see p.83)	Gr	Tobit 12.1, 5–15, 20 or Jude 17, 20–end Psalm 103.1, 8–13 or 63.1–6 Mark 12.38–end	Psalms 20, 21, **23** Job 12 Romans 6.15–end	Psalms **24**, 25 Joshua 10.1–15 Luke 11.37–end

Trinity 1

		Principal Service	3rd Service	2nd Service

Sunday	**6 June**
	1st Sunday after Trinity
	Proper 5
	
	G
		Continuous:
		1 Samuel 8.4–11 [12–15]
		16–20 [11.14–end]
		Psalm 138
		     Related:
		     Genesis 3.8–15
		     Psalm 130
		2 Corinthians 4.13—5.1
		Mark 3.20–end
			Morning Prayer
			Psalm 36
			Deuteronomy 6.10–end
			Acts 22.22—23.11
				Evening Prayer
				Psalm 37.1–11 [12–17]
				Jeremiah 6.16–21
				Romans 9.1–13
				HC Luke 7.11–17

Monday	**7 June** DEL week 10 G	**Holy Communion** 2 Corinthians 1.1–7 Psalm 34.1–8 Matthew 5.1–12	**Morning Prayer** Psalms 27, **30** Job 13 Romans 7.1–6	**Evening Prayer** Psalms 26, **28**, 29 Joshua 14 Luke 12.1–12
Tuesday	**8 June** Thomas Ken, bishop, nonjuror, hymn writer, 1711 (see p.85) Gw	2 Corinthians 1.18–22 Psalm 119.129–136 Matthew 5.13–16	Psalms 32, **36** Job 14 Romans 7.7–end	Psalm 33 Joshua 21.43—22.8 Luke 12.13–21
Wednesday	**9 June** Columba, abbot, missionary, 597 (see p.86) *Ephrem, deacon, hymn writer, teacher* *of the faith, 373* Gw	2 Corinthians 3.4–11 Psalm 78.1–4 Matthew 5.17–19	Psalm 34 Job 15 Romans 8.1–11	Psalm 119.33–56 Joshua 22.9–end Luke 12.22–31

Thursday	**10 June**
	
	G
		2 Corinthians 3.15—4.1, 3–6
		Psalm 78.36–40
		Matthew 5.20–26
			Psalm 37*
			Job 16.1—17.2
			Romans 8.12–17
				Psalms 39, 40
				Joshua 23
				Luke 12.32–40
				or: 1st EP of Barnabas the Apostle:
				     Psalms 1, 15;
				     Isaiah 42.5–12;
				     Acts 14.8–end

		Principal Service	**3rd Service**	**2nd Service**
Friday	**11 June** Barnabas the Apostle R	Job 29.11–16 or Acts 11.19–end Psalm 112 Acts 11.19–end or Galatians 2.1–10 John 15.12–17	MP Psalms 100, 101, 117 Jeremiah 9.23–24 Acts 4.32–end	EP Psalm 147 Ecclesiastes 12.9–end or Tobit 4.5–11 Acts 9.26–31
		Holy Communion	**Morning Prayer**	**Evening Prayer**
Saturday	**12 June** G	2 Corinthians 5.14–end Psalm 103.1–12 Matthew 5.33–37	Psalms 41, **42**, 43 Job 18 Romans 8.31–end	Psalms 45, **46** Joshua 24.29–end Luke 12.49–end

Trinity 2

	Principal Service	3rd Service	2nd Service
Sunday G	*Continuous:* 1 Samuel 15.34—16.13 Psalm 20 *Related:* Ezekiel 17.22-end Psalm 92.1-4, 12-end [or 92.1-8] 2 Corinthians 5.6-10 [11-13] 14-17 Mark 4.26-34	Psalms 42, 43 Deuteronomy 10.12—11.1 Acts 23.12-35	Psalm 39 Jeremiah 7.1-16 Romans 9.14-26 HC Luke 7.36—8.3
13 June 2nd Sunday after Trinity Proper 6			

	Holy Communion	Morning Prayer	Evening Prayer
Monday 14 June G *Richard Baxter, puritan divine, 1691* DEL week 11	2 Corinthians 6.1-10 Psalm 98 Matthew 5.38-42	Psalm **44** Job 19 Romans 9.1-18	Psalms **47**, 49 Judges 2 Luke 13.1-9
Tuesday 15 June G *Evelyn Underhill, spiritual writer, 1941*	2 Corinthians 8.1-9 Psalm 146 Matthew 5.43-end	Psalms **48**, 52 Job 21 Romans 9.19-end	Psalm **50** Judges 4.1-23 Luke 13.10-21
Wednesday 16 June Gw *Richard, bishop, 1253 (see p.85)* *Joseph Butler, bishop, philosopher, 1752*	2 Corinthians 9.6-11 Psalm 112 Matthew 6.1-6, 16-18	Psalm 119.**57-80** Job 22 Romans 10.1-10	Psalms **59**, 60 (67) Judges 5 Luke 13.22-end
Thursday 17 June G *Samuel and Henrietta Barnett, social reformers, 1913 and 1936*	2 Corinthians 11.1-11 Psalm 111 Matthew 6.7-15	Psalms 56, **57** (63*) Job 23 Romans 10.11-end	Psalms 61, **62**, 64 Judges 6.1-24 Luke 14.1-11
Friday 18 June G *Bernard Mizeki, martyr, 1896*	2 Corinthians 11.18, 21b-30 Psalm 34.1-6 Matthew 6.19-23	Psalms **51**, 54 Job 24 Romans 11.1-12	Psalm **38** Judges 6.25-end Luke 14.12-24
Saturday 19 June G *Sundar Singh, sadhu (holy man), evangelist, teacher of the faith, 1929*	2 Corinthians 12.1-10 Psalm 89.20-33 Matthew 6.24-end	Psalm **68** Job 25—26 Romans 11.13-24	Psalms 65, **66** Judges 7 Luke 14.25-end

	Principal Service	3rd Service	2nd Service
Sunday 20 June **3rd Sunday after Trinity** Proper 7 — G	*Continuous:* 1 Samuel 17. [1a, 4–11, 19–23] 32–49 Psalm 9.9–end or 1 Samuel 17.57—18.5, 10–16 Psalm 133 / *Related:* Job 38.1–11 Psalm 107.1–3, 23–32 [or 107.23–32] 2 Corinthians 6.1–13 Mark 4.35–41	Psalm 48 Deuteronomy 11.1–15 Acts 27.1–12	Psalm 49 Jeremiah 10.1–16 Romans 11.25–36 HC Luke 8.26–39

	Holy Communion	Morning Prayer	Evening Prayer
Monday 21 June DEL week 12 — G	Genesis 12.1–9 Psalm 33.12–end Matthew 7.1–5	Psalm **71** Job 27 Romans 11.25–end	Psalms **72**, 75 Judges 8.22–end Luke 15.1–10
Tuesday 22 June Alban, first martyr of Britain, c.250 (see p.83) — Gr	Genesis 13.2, 5–end Psalm 15 Matthew 7.6, 12–14	Psalm **73** Job 28 Romans 12.1–8	Psalm **74** Judges 9.1–21 Luke 15.1–end
Wednesday 23 June Etheldreda, abbess, c.678 (see p.86) Ember Day — Gw	Genesis 15.1–12, 17–18 Psalm 105.1–9 Matthew 7.15–20	Psalm **77** Job 29 Romans 12.9–end	Psalm **119.81–104** Judges 9.22–end Luke 16.1–18 *or:* 1st EP of the Birth of John the Baptist: Psalm 71; Judges 13.2–7, 24–end; Luke 1.5–25

	Principal Service	3rd Service	2nd Service
Thursday 24 June Birth of John the Baptist — W	Isaiah 40.1–11 Psalm 85.7–end Acts 13.14b–26 or Galatians 3.23–end Luke 1.57–66, 80	MP Psalms 50, 149 Ecclesiasticus 48.1–10 or Malachi 3.1–6 Luke 3.1–17	EP Psalms 80, 82 Malachi 4 Matthew 11.2–19

	Holy Communion	Morning Prayer	Evening Prayer
Friday 25 June Ember Day — G	Genesis 17.1, 9–10, 15–22 Psalm 128 Matthew 8.1–4	Psalm **55** Job 31 Romans 13.8–end	Psalm **69** Judges 11.29–end Luke 17.1–10
Saturday 26 June Ember Day — G	Genesis 18.1–15 Canticle: Luke 1.46b–55 Matthew 8.5–17	Psalms **76**, 79 Job 32 Romans 14.1–12	Psalms 81, **84** Judges 12.1–7 Luke 17.11–19

Trinity 4

	Principal Service	3rd Service	2nd Service
Sunday 27 June G **4th Sunday after Trinity** Proper 8	*Continuous:* 2 Samuel 1.1,17-end Psalm 130 *Related:* Wisdom 1.13–15; 2.23–24 *Canticle:* †Lamentations 3.23–33 or Psalm 30 †*Lamentations 3.23–33 may be read as the first reading in place of Wisdom 1.13–15; 2.23,24* 2 Corinthians 8.7–end Mark 5.21–end	Psalm 56 Deuteronomy 15.1–11 Acts 27.[13–32] 33–end	Psalms [52] 53 Jeremiah 11.1–14 Romans 13.1–10 HC Luke 9.51–62

	Holy Communion	Morning Prayer	Evening Prayer
Monday 28 June Gw Irenaeus, bishop, teacher of the faith, c.200 (see p.84) DEL week 13	Genesis 18.16–end Psalm 103.6–17 Matthew 8.18–22	Psalms **80**, 82 Job 33 Romans 14.13–end	Psalms **85**, 86 Judges 13.1–24 Luke 17.20–end *or:* 1st EP of Peter and Paul, Apostles [or †Peter the Apostle alone]: Psalms 66, 67; Ezekiel 3.4–11; Galatians 1.13—2.8 [†Acts 9.32–end]

	Principal Service	3rd Service	2nd Service
Tuesday 29 June R Peter and Paul, Apostles or Peter the Apostle R	*Peter and Paul:* Zechariah 4.1–6a, 10b–end or Acts 12.1–11 Psalm 125 Acts 12.1–11 or 2 Timothy 4.6–8, 17–18 Matthew 16.13–19 *Peter alone:* Ezekiel 3.22–end or Acts 12.1–11 Psalm 125 Acts 12.1–11 or 1 Peter 2.19–end Matthew 16.13–19	MP Psalms 71, 113 Isaiah 49.1–6 Acts 11.1–18	EP Psalms 124, 138 Ezekiel 34.11–16 John 21.15–22

Trinity 4

		Holy Communion	Morning Prayer	Evening Prayer
Wednesday 30 June	G	Genesis 21.5, 8–20 Psalm 34.1–12 Matthew 8.28–end	Psalm 119.105–128 Job 39 Romans 15.14–21	Psalms 91, 93 Judges 15.1—16.3 Luke 18.15–30
Thursday 1 July *Henry, John, and Henry Venn, priests,* *evangelical divines, 1797, 1813, 1873*	G	Genesis 22.1–19 Psalm 116.1–7 Matthew 9.1–8	Psalms 90, 92 Job 40 Romans 15.22–end	Psalm 94 Judges 16.4–end Luke 18.31–end
Friday 2 July	G	Genesis 23.1–4, 19, 24.1–8, 62–end Psalm 106.1–5 Matthew 9.9–13	Psalms 88 (95) Job 41 Romans 16.1–16	Psalm 102 Judges 17 Luke 19.1–10 *or:* 1st EP of Thomas the Apostle: Psalm 27; Isaiah 35; Hebrews 10.35—11.1

		Principal Service	3rd Service	2nd Service
Saturday 3 July Thomas the Apostle	R	Habakkuk 2.1–4 Psalm 31.1–6 Ephesians 2.19–end John 20.24–29	MP Psalms 92, 146 2 Samuel 15.17–21 or Ecclesiasticus 2 John 11.1–16	EP Psalm 139 Job 42.1–6 1 Peter 1.3–12

Trinity 5

		Principal Service		3rd Service	2nd Service
Sunday 4 July **5th Sunday after Trinity** Proper 9	G	*Continuous:* 2 Samuel 5.1–5, 9–10 Psalm 48	*Related:* Ezekiel 2.1–5 Psalm 123 2 Corinthians 12.2–10 Mark 6.1–13	Psalm 57 Deuteronomy 24.10–end Acts 28.1–16	Psalms [63] 64 Jeremiah 20.1–11a Romans 14.1–17 HC Luke 10.1–11, 16–20
		Holy Communion		**Morning Prayer**	**Evening Prayer**
Monday 5 July DEL week 14	G	Genesis 28.10–end Psalm 91.1–10 Matthew 9.18–26		Psalms **98**, 99, 101 Ezekiel 1.1–14 2 Corinthians 1.1–14	Psalms **105*** (or 103) 1 Samuel 1.1–20 Luke 19.28–40
Tuesday 6 July *Thomas More, scholar, and John Fisher, bishop, martyrs, 1535*	G	Genesis 32.22–end Psalm 17.1–8 Matthew 9.32–end		Psalm **106*** (or 103) Ezekiel 1.15—2.2 2 Corinthians 1.15—2.4	Psalms **107*** 1 Samuel 1.21—2.11 Luke 19.41–end
Wednesday 7 July	G	Genesis 41.55–end, 42.5–7, 17–end Psalm 33.1–4, 18–end Matthew 10.1–7		Psalms 110, **111**, 112 Ezekiel 2.3—3.11 2 Corinthians 2.5–end	Psalm **119.129–152** 1 Samuel 2.12–26 Luke 20.1–8
Thursday 8 July	G	Genesis 44.18–21, 23–29, 45.1–5 Psalm 105.11–17 Matthew 10.7–15		Psalms 113, **115** Ezekiel 3.12–end 2 Corinthians 3	Psalms 114, **116**, 117 1 Samuel 2.27–end Luke 20.9–19
Friday 9 July	G	Genesis 46.1–7, 28–30 Psalm 37.3–6, 27–28 Matthew 10.16–23		Psalm **139** Ezekiel 8 2 Corinthians 4	Psalms **130**, 131, 137 1 Samuel 3.1—4.1a Luke 20.20–26
Saturday 10 July	G	Genesis 49.29–end, 50.15–25 Psalm 105.1–7 Matthew 10.24–33		Psalms 120, **121**, 122 Ezekiel 9 2 Corinthians 5	Psalm **118** 1 Samuel 4.1b–end Luke 20.27–40

Trinity 6

		Principal Service		3rd Service	2nd Service
Sunday	**11 July** G **6th Sunday after Trinity** Proper 10	*Continuous:* 2 Samuel 6.1–5, 12b–19 Psalm 24	*Related:* Amos 7.7–15 Psalm 85.8–end Ephesians 1.3–14 Mark 6.14–29	Psalm 65 Deuteronomy 28.1–14 Acts 28.17–end	Psalm 66 [or 66.1–8] Job 4.1; 5.6–end or Ecclesiasticus 4.11–end Romans 15.14–29 HC Luke 10.25–37
		Holy Communion		**Morning Prayer**	**Evening Prayer**
Monday	**12 July** G DEL week 15	Exodus 1.8–14, 22 Psalm 124 Matthew 10.34—11.1		Psalms 123, 124, 125, **126** Ezekiel 10.1–19 2 Corinthians 6.1—7.1	Psalms **127**, 128, 129 1 Samuel 5 Luke 20.41—21.4
Tuesday	**13 July** G	Exodus 2.1–15 Psalm 69.1–2, 31–end Matthew 11.20–24		Psalms **132**, 133 Ezekiel 11.14–end 2 Corinthians 7.2–end	Psalms (134) **135** 1 Samuel 6.1–16 Luke 21.5–19
Wednesday	**14 July** Gw John Keble, priest, poet, 1866 (see p.85)	Exodus 3.1–6, 9–12 Psalm 103.1–7 Matthew 11.25–27		Psalm 1 19.**153–end** Ezekiel 12.1–16 2 Corinthians 8.1–15	Psalm **136** 1 Samuel 7 Luke 21.20–28
Thursday	**15 July** Gw Swithun, bishop, c.862 (see p.85) *Bonaventure, friar, bishop,* *teacher of the faith, 1274*	Exodus 3.13–20 Psalm 105.1–2, 23 Matthew 11.28–end		Psalms **143**, 146 Ezekiel 12.17–end 2 Corinthians 8.16—9.5	Psalms **138**, 140, 141 1 Samuel 8 Luke 21.29–end
Friday	**16 July** G *Osmund, bishop, 1099*	Exodus 11.10—12.14 Psalm 116.10–end Matthew 12.1–8		Psalms 142, **144** Ezekiel 13.1–16 2 Corinthians 9.6–end	Psalm **145** 1 Samuel 9.1–14 Luke 22.1–13
Saturday	**17 July** G	Exodus 12.37–42 Psalm 136.1–4, 10–15 Matthew 12.14–21		Psalm **147** Ezekiel 14.1–11 2 Corinthians 10	Psalms **148**, 149, 150 1 Samuel 9.15—10.1 Luke 22.14–23

			Principal Service	3rd Service	2nd Service
Sunday	**18 July** **7th Sunday after Trinity** Proper 11	G	*Continuous:* 2 Samuel 7.1–14a Psalm 89.20–37 *Related:* Jeremiah 23.1–6 Psalm 23 Ephesians 2.11–end Mark 6.30–34, 53–end	Psalms 67, 70 Deuteronomy 30.1–10 1 Peter 3.8–18	Psalm 73 [or 73.21–end] Job 13.13—14.6 or Ecclesiasticus 18.1–14 Hebrews 2.5–end HC Luke 10.38–end

			Holy Communion	Morning Prayer	Evening Prayer
Monday	**19 July** *Gregory, bishop, and his sister Macrina, deaconess, teachers of the faith, c.394 and c.379 (see p.84)* DEL week 16	Gw	Exodus 14.5–18 Psalm 136.1–4, 10–15 or Canticle: Exodus 15.1–6 Matthew 12.38–42	Psalms 1, 2, 3 Ezekiel 14.12–end 2 Corinthians 11.1–15	Psalms **4**, 7 1 Samuel 10.1–16 Luke 22.24–30
Tuesday	**20 July** *Margaret of Antioch, martyr, 4th cent.* *Bartolomé de las Casas, Apostle to the Indies, 1566*	G	Exodus 14.21—15.1 Psalm 105.37–44 or Canticle: Exodus 15.8–10, 12, 17 Matthew 12.46–end	Psalms **5**, 6, (8) Ezekiel 18.1–20 2 Corinthians 11.16–end	Psalms **9**, 10 1 Samuel 10.17–end Luke 22.31–38

			Principal Service	3rd Service	2nd Service
Wednesday	**21 July**	G	Exodus 16.1–5, 9–15 Psalm 78.17–31 Matthew 13.1–9	Psalm **119.1–32** Ezekiel 18.21–32 2 Corinthians 12	Psalms **11**, 12, 13 1 Samuel 11 Luke 22.39–46 *or:* 1st EP of Mary Magdalene: Psalm 139; Isaiah 25.1–9; 2 Corinthians 1.3–7
Thursday	**22 July** Mary Magdalene	W	Song of Solomon 3.1–4 Psalm 42.1–10 2 Corinthians 5.14–17 John 20.1–2, 11–18	MP Psalms 30, 32, 150 1 Samuel 16.14–end Luke 8.1–3	EP Psalm 63 Zephaniah 3.14–end Mark 15.40—16.7

			Holy Communion	Morning Prayer	Evening Prayer
Friday	**23 July** *Bridget, abbess, 1373*	G	Exodus 20.1–17 Psalm 19.7–11 Matthew 13.18–23	Psalms 17, **19** Ezekiel 20.21–38 James 1.1–11	Psalm **22** 1 Samuel 13.5–18 Luke 22.63–end
Saturday	**24 July**	G	Exodus 24.3–8 Psalm 50.1–6, 14–15 Matthew 13.24–30	Psalms 20, 21, **23** Ezekiel 24.15–end James 1.12–end	Psalms **24**, 25 1 Samuel 13.19—14.15 Luke 23.1–12 *or, if James the Apostle is celebrated on 25 July:* 1st EP of James the Apostle: Psalm 144; Deuteronomy 30.11–end; Mark 5.21–end

James / Trinity 8

If James the Apostle is celebrated on Sunday 25 July:

	Principal Service	3rd Service	2nd Service
Sunday **25 July** James the Apostle R	Jeremiah 45.1–5 or Acts 11.27—12.2 Psalm 126 Acts 11.27—12.2 or 2 Corinthians 4.7–15 Matthew 20.20–28	MP Psalms 7, 29, 117 2 Kings 1.9–15 Luke 9.46–56	EP Psalm 94 Jeremiah 26.1–15 Mark 1.14–20

	Holy Communion	Morning Prayer	Evening Prayer
Monday **26 July** Anne and Joachim, parents of the Blessed Virgin Mary DEL week 17 Gw	Exodus 32.15–24, 30–34 Psalm 106.19–23 Matthew 13.31–35 *Lesser Festival eucharistic lectionary:* Zephaniah 3.14–18a Psalm 127 Romans 8.28–30 Matthew 13.16–17	Psalms 27, **30** Ezekiel 28.1–19 James 2.1–13	Psalms 26, **28**, 29 1 Samuel 14.24–46 Luke 23.13–25

If James the Apostle is transferred to Monday 26 July:

	Principal Service		3rd Service	2nd Service
Sunday **25 July** 8th Sunday after Trinity Proper 12 G	*Continuous:* 2 Samuel 11.1–15 Psalm 14	*Related:* 2 Kings 4.42–end Psalm 145.10–19 Ephesians 3.14–end John 6.1–21	Psalm 75 Song of Solomon 2 or 1 Maccabees 2.[1–14] 15–22 1 Peter 4.7–14	Psalm 74 [or 74.11–16] Job 19.1–27a or Ecclesiasticus 38.24–end Hebrews 8 HC Luke 11.1–13 or: 1st EP of James the Apostle: Psalm 144; Deuteronomy 30.11–end; Mark 5.21–end

	Principal Service	3rd Service	2nd Service
Monday **26 July** James the Apostle *(transferred from 25 July)* R	Jeremiah 45.1–5 or Acts 11.27—12.2 Psalm 126 Acts 11.27—12.2 or 2 Corinthians 4.7–15 Matthew 20.20–28	MP Psalms 7, 29, 117 2 Kings 1.9–15 Luke 9.46–56	EP Psalm 94 Jeremiah 26.1–15 Mark 1.14–20

Trinity 8

		Holy Communion	Morning Prayer	Evening Prayer
Tuesday 27 July G *Brooke Foss Westcott, bishop, teacher of the faith, 1901* DEL week 17		Exodus 33.7–11, 34.5–9, 28 Psalm 103.8–12 Matthew 13.36–43	Psalms 32, **36** Ezekiel 33.1–20 James 2.14–end	Psalm **33** 1 Samuel 15.1–23 Luke 23.26–43
Wednesday 28 July G		Exodus 34.29–end Psalm 99 Matthew 13.44–46	Psalm **34** Ezekiel 33.21–end James 3	Psalm 11**9.33–56** 1 Samuel 16 Luke 23.44–56*a*
Thursday 29 July Gw *Mary, Martha and Lazarus, companions of Our Lord*		Exodus 40.16–21, 34–end Psalm 84.1–6 Matthew 13.47–53 *Lesser Festival eucharistic lectionary:* Isaiah 25.6–9 Psalm 49.5–10, 16 Hebrews 2.10–15 John 12.1–8	Psalm **37*** Ezekiel 34.1–16 James 4.1–12	Psalms 39, **40** 1 Samuel 17.1–30 Luke 23.56*b*—24.12
Friday 30 July Gw *William Wilberforce, social reformer, Olaudah Equiano and Thomas Clarkson, anti-slavery campaigners, 1833, 1797 and 1846 (see p.87)*		Leviticus 23.1, 4–11, 15–16, 27, 34–37 Psalm 81.1–8 Matthew 13.54–end	Psalm **31** Ezekiel 34.17–end James 4.13—5.6	Psalm **35** 1 Samuel 17.31–54 Luke 24.13–35
Saturday 31 July G *Ignatius of Loyola, founder of the Society of Jesus, 1556*		Leviticus 25.1, 8–17 Psalm 67 Matthew 14.1–12	Psalms 41, **42**, 43 Ezekiel 36.16–36 James 5.7–end	Psalms 45, **46** 1 Samuel 17.55—18.16 Luke 24.36–end

	Principal Service	3rd Service	2nd Service
Sunday 1 August G **9th Sunday after Trinity** Proper 13	*Continuous:* 2 Samuel 11.26—12.13a Psalm 51.1–13 *Related:* Exodus 16.2–4, 9–15 Psalm 78.23–29 Ephesians 4.1–16 John 6.24–35	Psalm 86 Song of Solomon 5.2–end or 1 Maccabees 3.1–12 2 Peter 1.1–15	Psalm 88 [or 88.1–10] Job 28 or Ecclesiasticus 42.15–end Hebrews 11.17–31 HC Luke 12.13–21
	Holy Communion	**Morning Prayer**	**Evening Prayer**
Monday 2 August G DEL week 18	Numbers 11.4–15 Psalm 81.1–end Matthew 14.13–21 or 14.22–end	Psalm 44 Ezekiel 37.1–14 Mark 1.1–13	Psalms **47**, 49 1 Samuel 19.1–18 Acts 1.1–14
Tuesday 3 August G	Numbers 12.1–13 Psalm 51.1–8 Matthew 14.22–end or 15.1–2, 10–14	Psalms **48**, 52 Ezekiel 37.15–end Mark 1.14–20	Psalm 50 1 Samuel 20.1–17 Acts 1.15–end
Wednesday 4 August G *Jean-Baptiste Vianney, curé d'Ars,* *spiritual guide, 1859*	Numbers 13.1–2, 25–14.1, 26–35 Psalm 106.14–24 Matthew 15.21–28	Psalm 119.**57–80** Ezekiel 39.21–end Mark 1.21–28	Psalms **59**, 60 (67) 1 Samuel 20.18–end Acts 2.1–21
Thursday 5 August Gr *Oswald, king, martyr, 642 (see p.83)*	Numbers 20.1–13 Psalm 95.1, 8–end Matthew 16.13–23	Psalms 56, **57** (63*) Ezekiel 43.1–12 Mark 1.29–end	Psalms 61, **62**, 64 1 Samuel 21.1–22.5 Acts 2.22–36 *or:* 1st EP of the Transfiguration of Our Lord: Psalms 99, 110; Exodus 24.12–end; John 12.27–36a
	Principal Service	**3rd Service**	**2nd Service**
Friday 6 August *Gold or W* Transfiguration of Our Lord	Daniel 7.9–10, 13–14 Psalm 97 2 Peter 1.16–19 Luke 9.28–36	MP Psalms 27, 150 Ecclesiasticus 48.1–10 or 1 Kings 19.1–16 1 John 3.1–3	EP Psalm 72 Exodus 34.29–end 2 Corinthians 3
	Holy Communion	**Morning Prayer**	**Evening Prayer**
Saturday 7 August G *John Mason Neale, priest, hymn writer, 1866*	Deuteronomy 6.4–13 Psalm 18.1–2, 48–end Matthew 17.14–20	Psalm 68 Ezekiel 47.1–12 Mark 2.13–22	Psalms 65, **66** 1 Samuel 23 Acts 3.1–10

		Principal Service	3rd Service	2nd Service
Sunday	**8 August** **10th Sunday after Trinity** Proper 14	G	*Continuous:* 2 Samuel 18.5–9, 15, 31–33 Psalm 130 *Related:* 1 Kings 19.4–8 Psalm 34.1–8 Ephesians 4.25—5.2 John 6.35, 41–51	Psalm 90 Song of Solomon 8.5–7 or 1 Maccabees 14.4–15 2 Peter 3.8–13	Psalm 91 [or 91.1–[12] Job 39.1—40.4 or Ecclesiasticus 43.13–end Hebrews 12.1–17 HC Luke 12.32–40
			Holy Communion	**Morning Prayer**	**Evening Prayer**
Monday	**9 August** Mary Sumner, founder of the Mothers' Union, 1921 (see p.87) DEL week 19	Gw	Deuteronomy 10.12–end Psalm 147.13–end Matthew 17.22–end	Psalm 71 Proverbs 1.1–19 Mark 2.23—3.6	Psalms **72**, 75 1 Samuel 24 Acts 3.11–end
Tuesday	**10 August** Laurence, deacon, martyr, 258 (see p.83)	Gr	Deuteronomy 31.1–8 Psalm 107.1–3, 42–end or *Canticle:* Deuteronomy 32.3–4, 7–9 Matthew 18.1–5, 10, 12–14	Psalm 73 Proverbs 1.20–end Mark 3.7–19a	Psalm **74** 1 Samuel 26 Acts 4.1–12
Wednesday	**11 August** Clare of Assisi, founder of the Poor Clares, 1253 (see p.86) *John Henry Newman, priest, 1890*	Gw	Deuteronomy 34 Psalm 66.14–end Matthew 18.15–20	Psalm 77 Proverbs 2 Mark 3.19b–end	Psalm **119.81–104** 1 Samuel 28.3–end Acts 4.13–31
Thursday	**12 August**	G	Joshua 3.7–11, 13–17 Psalm 114 Matthew 18.21—19.1	Psalm **78.1–39*** Proverbs 3.1–26 Mark 4.1–20	Psalm **78.40–end*** 1 Samuel 31 Acts 4.32—5.11
Friday	**13 August** Jeremy Taylor, bishop, teacher of the faith, 1667 (see p.84) *Florence Nightingale, nurse, social reformer, 1910 Octavia Hill, social reformer, 1912*	Gw	Joshua 24.1–13 Psalm 136.1–3, 16–22 Matthew 19.3–12	Psalm **55** Proverbs 3.27—4.19 Mark 4.21–34	Psalm **69** 2 Samuel 1 Acts 5.12–26
Saturday	**14 August** *Maximilian Kolbe, friar, martyr, 1941*	G	Joshua 24.14–29 Psalm 16.1, 5–end Matthew 19.13–15	Psalms **76**, 79 Proverbs 6.1–19 Mark 4.35–end	Psalms 81, **84** 2 Samuel 2.1–11 Acts 5.27–end *Or, if The Blessed Virgin Mary is celebrated on 15 August:* 1st EP of the Blessed Virgin Mary: Psalm 72; Proverbs 8.22–31; John 19.23–27

The Blessed Virgin Mary / Trinity 11

If The Blessed Virgin Mary is celebrated on Sunday 15 August:

		Principal Service	3rd Service	2nd Service
Sunday	**15 August** W The Blessed Virgin Mary	Isaiah 61.10-end or Revelation 11.19—12.6, 10 Psalm 45.10-end Galatians 4.4-7 Luke 1.46-55	MP Psalms 98, 138, 147.1-12 Isaiah 7.10-15 Luke 11.27-28	EP Psalm 132 Song of Solomon 2.1-7 Acts 1.6-14
		Holy Communion	**Morning Prayer**	**Evening Prayer**
Monday	**16 August** G DEL week 20	Judges 2.11-19 Psalm 106.34-42 Matthew 19.16-22	Psalms 80, 82 Proverbs 8.1-21 Mark 5.1-20	Psalms **85**, 86 2 Samuel 3.12-end Acts 6

If The Blessed Virgin Mary is transferred to Monday 16 August:

		Principal Service	3rd Service	2nd Service
Sunday	**15 August** G **11th Sunday after Trinity** Proper 15	*Continuous:* 1 Kings 2.10-12; 3.3-14 Psalm 111 *Related:* Proverbs 9.1-6 Psalm 34.9-14 Ephesians 5.15-20 John 6.51-58	Psalm 106.1-10 Jonah 1 or Ecclesiasticus 3.1-15 2 Peter 3.14-end	Psalms [92] 100 Exodus 2.23—3.10 Hebrews 13.1-15 HC Luke 12.49-56 *or:* 1st EP of the Blessed Virgin Mary: Psalm 72; Proverbs 8.22-31; John 19.23-27
Monday	**16 August** W The Blessed Virgin Mary *(transferred from 15 August)*	Isaiah 61.10-end or Revelation 11.19—12.6, 10 Psalm 45.10-end Galatians 4.4-7 Luke 1.46-55	MP Psalms 98, 138, 147.1-12 Isaiah 7.10-15 Luke 11.27-28	EP Psalm 132 Song of Solomon 2.1-7 Acts 1.6-14

Trinity 11

		Holy Communion	Morning Prayer	Evening Prayer
Tuesday	**17 August** DEL week 20	G	Judges 6.11–24 Psalm 85.8–end Matthew 19.23–end	Psalms 87, **89.1–18** Proverbs 8.22–end Mark 5.21–34	Psalm **89.19–end** 2 Samuel 5.1–12 Acts 7.1–16
Wednesday	**18 August**	G	Judges 9.6–15 Psalm 21.1–6 Matthew 20.1–16	Psalm **119.105–128** Proverbs 9 Mark 5.35–end	Psalms **91**, 93 2 Samuel 6.1–19 Acts 7.17–43
Thursday	**19 August**	G	Judges 11.29–end Psalm 40.4–11 Matthew 22.1–14	Psalms 90, **92** Proverbs 10.1–12 Mark 6.1–13	Psalm **94** 2 Samuel 7.1–17 Acts 7.44–53
Friday	**20 August** Gw Bernard, abbot, teacher of the faith, 1153 (see p.84) *William and Catherine Booth,* *founders of the Salvation Army, 1912, 1890*		Ruth 1.1, 3–6, 14–16, 22 Psalm 146 Matthew 22.34–40	Psalms **88** (95) Proverbs 11.1–12 Mark 6.14–29	Psalm **102** 2 Samuel 7.18–end Acts 7.54—8.3
Saturday	**21 August**	G	Ruth 2.1–3, 8–11, 4.13–17 Psalm 128 Matthew 23.1–12	Psalms 96, **97**, 100 Proverbs 12.10–end Mark 6.30–44	Psalm **104** 2 Samuel 9 Acts 8.4–25

		Principal Service		3rd Service	2nd Service
Sunday	**22 August** **12th Sunday after Trinity** Proper 16	G	Continuous: 1 Kings 8.[1, 6, 10–11] 22–30, 41–43 Psalm 84	Related: Joshua 24.1–2a, 14–18 Psalm 34.15–end Ephesians 6.10–20 John 6.56–69	Psalm 115 Jonah 2 or Ecclesiasticus 3.17–29 Revelation 1	Psalm 116 [or 116.10–end] Exodus 4.27—5.1 Hebrews 13.16–21 HC Luke 13.10–17

			Holy Communion	Morning Prayer	Evening Prayer
Monday	**23 August** DEL week 21	G		1 Thessalonians 1.1–5, 8–end Psalm 149.1–5 Matthew 23.13–22	Psalms 98, 99, 101 Proverbs 14.31—15.17 Mark 6.45–end	Psalm 105* (or 103) 2 Samuel 11 Acts 8.26–end or: 1st EP of Bartholomew the Apostle: Psalm 97; Isaiah 61.1–9; 2 Corinthians 6.1–10

			Principal Service	3rd Service	2nd Service
Tuesday	**24 August** Bartholomew the Apostle	R		Isaiah 43.8–13 or Acts 5.12–16 Psalm 145.1–7 Acts 5.12–16 or 1 Corinthians 4.9–15 Luke 22.24–30	MP Psalms 86, 117 Genesis 28.10–17 John 1.43–end	EP Psalms 91, 116 Ecclesiasticus 39.1–10 or Deuteronomy 18.15–19 Matthew 10.1–22

			Holy Communion	Morning Prayer	Evening Prayer
Wednesday	**25 August**	G		1 Thessalonians 2.9–13 Psalm 126 Matthew 23.27–32	Psalms 110, 111, 112 Proverbs 18.10–end Mark 7.14–23	Psalm 119.129–152 2 Samuel 15.1–12 Acts 9.19b–31
Thursday	**26 August**	G		1 Thessalonians 3.7–end Psalm 90.13–end Matthew 24.42–end	Psalms 113, 115 Proverbs 20.1–22 Mark 7.24–30	Psalms 114, 116, 117 2 Samuel 15.13–end Acts 9.32–end
Friday	**27 August** Monica, mother of Augustine of Hippo, 387 (see p.87)	Gw		1 Thessalonians 4.1–8 Psalm 97 Matthew 25.1–13	Psalm 139 Proverbs 22.1–16 Mark 7.31–end	Psalms 130, 131, 137 2 Samuel 16.1–14 Acts 10.1–16
Saturday	**28 August** Augustine, bishop, teacher of the faith, 430 (see p.84)	Gw		1 Thessalonians 4.9–12 Psalm 98.1–2, 8–end Matthew 25.14–30	Psalms 120, 121, 122 Proverbs 24.23–end Mark 8.1–10	Psalm 118 2 Samuel 17.1–23 Acts 10.17–33

Trinity 13

	Principal Service	3rd Service	2nd Service
Sunday **29 August** 13th Sunday after Trinity Proper 17 — G	*Continuous:* Song of Solomon 2.8–13 Psalm 45.1–2, 6–9 [or 45.1–7] *Related:* Deuteronomy 4.1–2, 6–9 Psalm 15 James 1.17–end Mark 7.1–8, 14, 15,21–23	Psalm 119.17–40 Jonah 3.1–9 or Ecclesiasticus 11.7–28 (or 19–28) Revelation 3.14–end	Psalm 119.1–16 [or 119.9–16] Exodus 12.21–27 Matthew 4.23—5.20

	Holy Communion	Morning Prayer	Evening Prayer
Monday 30 August John Bunyan, spiritual writer, 1688 (see p.84) DEL week 22 — Gw	1 Thessalonians 4.13–end Psalm 96 Luke 4.16–30	Psalms 123, 124, 125, **126** Proverbs 25.1–14 Mark 8.11–21	Psalms **127**, 128, 129 2 Samuel 18.1–18 Acts 10.34–end
Tuesday 31 August Aidan, bishop, missionary, 651 (see p.86) — Gw	1 Thessalonians 5.1–6, 9–11 Psalm 27.1–8 Luke 4.31–37	Psalms **132**, 133 Proverbs 25.15–end Mark 8.22–26	Psalms (134) **135** 2 Samuel 18.19—19.8a Acts 11.1–18
Wednesday 1 September *Giles, hermit, c.710* — G	Colossians 1.1–8 Psalm 34.1–18 Luke 4.38–end	Psalm 119.**153–end** Proverbs 26.12–end Mark 8.27—9.1	Psalm **136** 2 Samuel 19.8b–23 Acts 11.19–end
Thursday 2 September *Martyrs of Papua New Guinea, 1901, 1942* — G	Colossians 1.9–14 Psalm 98.1–5 Luke 5.1–11	Psalms **143**, 146 Proverbs 27.1–22 Mark 9.2–13	Psalms **138**, 140, 141 2 Samuel 19.24–end Acts 12.1–17
Friday 3 September Gregory the Great, bishop, teacher of the faith, 604 (see p.84) — Gw	Colossians 1.15–20 Psalm 89.19b–28 Luke 5.33–end	Psalms 142, **144** Proverbs 30.1–9, 24–31 Mark 9.14–29	Psalm **145** 2 Samuel 23.1–7 Acts 12.18–end
Saturday 4 September *Birinus, bishop, 650* — G	Colossians 1.21–23 Psalm 117 Luke 6.1–5	Psalm **147** Proverbs 31.10–end Mark 9.30–37	Psalms **148**, 149, 150 2 Samuel 24 Acts 13.1–12

		Principal Service	3rd Service	2nd Service
		Holy Communion	Morning Prayer	Evening Prayer
Sunday	**5 September** G **14th Sunday after Trinity** Proper 18	*Continuous:* Proverbs 22.1-2, 8-9, 22-23 Psalm 125 *Related:* Isaiah 35.4-7a Psalm 146 James 2.1-10 [11-13] 14-17 Mark 7.24-end	Psalm 119.57-72 Jonah 3.10—4.11 or Ecclesiasticus 27.30—28.9 Revelation 8.1-5	Psalm 119.41-56 [or 119.49-56] Exodus 14.5-end Matthew 6.1-18
Monday	**6 September** G *Allen Gardiner, missionary, founder of the South American Mission Society, 1851* DEL week 23	Colossians 1.24—2.3 Psalm 62.1-7 Luke 6.6-11	Psalms 1, 2, 3 Wisdom 1 or 1 Chronicles 10.1—11.9 Mark 9.38-end	Psalms **4**, 7 1 Kings 1.5-31 Acts 13.13-43
Tuesday	**7 September** G	Colossians 2.6-15 Psalm 8 Luke 6.12-19	Psalms 5, 6 (8) Wisdom 2 or 1 Chronicles 13 Mark 10.1-16	Psalms **9**, 10* 1 Kings 1.32—2.4; 2.10-12 Acts 13.44—14.7
Wednesday	**8 September** Gw **Birth of the Blessed Virgin Mary** (see p.83)	Colossians 3.1-11 Psalm 15 Luke 6.20-26	Psalm 119.**1-32** Wisdom 3.1-9 or 1 Chronicles 15.1—16.3 Mark 10.17-31	Psalms 11, 12, 13 1 Kings 3 Acts 14.8-end
Thursday	**9 September** G *Charles Fuge Lowder, priest, 1880*	Colossians 3.12-17 Psalm 149.1-5 Luke 6.27-38	Psalms 14, **15**, 16 Wisdom 4.7-end or 1 Chronicles 17 Mark 10.32-34	Psalm 18* 1 Kings 4.29—5.12 Acts 15.1-21
Friday	**10 September** G	1 Timothy 1.1-2, 12-14 Psalm 16 Luke 6.39-42	Psalms 17, **19** Wisdom 5.1-16 or 1 Chronicles 21.1—22.1 Mark 10.35-45	Psalm **22** 1 Kings 6.1, 11-28 Acts 15.22-35
Saturday	**11 September** G	1 Timothy 1.15-17 Psalm 113 Luke 6.43-end	Psalms 20, 21, **23** Wisdom 5.17—6.11 or 1 Chronicles 22.2-end Mark 10.46-end	Psalms **24**, 25 1 Kings 8.1-30 Acts 15.36—16.5

Trinity 15

		Principal Service	3rd Service	2nd Service
Sunday	**12 September** **15th Sunday after Trinity** Proper 19 G	*Continuous:* Proverbs 1.20–33 Psalm 19 [or 19.1–6] *or Canticle:* Wisdom 7.26—8.1 *Related:* Isaiah 50.4–9*a* Psalm 116.1–8 James 3.1–12 Mark 8.27–end	Psalm 119.105–120 Isaiah 44.24—45.8 Revelation 12.1–12	Psalm 119.73–88 [or 119.73–80] Exodus 18.13–26 Matthew 7.1–14

		Holy Communion	Morning Prayer	Evening Prayer
Monday	**13 September** Gw John Chrysostom, bishop, teacher of the faith, 407 (see p.84) DEL week 24	1 Timothy 2.1–8 Psalm 28 Luke 7.1–10	Psalms 27, **30** Wisdom 6.12–23 *or* 1 Chronicles 28.1–10 Mark 11.1–11	Psalms 26, **28**, 29 1 Kings 8.31–62 Acts 16.6–24 *or:* 1st EP of Holy Cross Day: Psalm 66; Isaiah 52.13—end of 53; Ephesians 2.11–end

		Principal Service	3rd Service	2nd Service
Tuesday	**14 September** R Holy Cross Day	Numbers 21.4–9 Psalm 22.23–28 Philippians 2.6–11 John 3.13–17	MP Psalms 2, **8**, 146 Genesis 3.1–15 John 12.27–36*a*	EP Psalms 110, 150 Isaiah 63.1–16 1 Corinthians 1.18–25

		Holy Communion	Morning Prayer	Evening Prayer
Wednesday	**15 September** Gr Cyprian, bishop, martyr, 258 (see p.83)	1 Timothy 3.14–end Psalm 111.1–5 Luke 7.31–35	Psalm **34** Wisdom 7.15—8.4 *or* 1 Chronicles 29.1–9 Mark 11.27–end	Psalm **119.33–56** 1 Kings 10.1–25 Acts 17.1–15
Thursday	**16 September** Gw Ninian, bishop, apostle of the Picts, c.432 (see p.86) *Edward Bouverie Pusey, priest, 1882*	1 Timothy 4.12–end Psalm 111.6–end Luke 7.36–end	Psalm **37*** Wisdom 8.5–18 *or* 1 Chronicles 29.10–20 Mark 12.1–12	Psalms 39, **40** 1 Kings 11.1–13 Acts 17.16–end
Friday	**17 September** Gw Hildegard, abbess, visionary, 1179 (see p.86)	1 Timothy 6.2*b*–12 Psalm 49.1–9 Luke 8.1–3	Psalm **31** Wisdom 8.21—end of 9 *or* 1 Chronicles 29.21–end Mark 12.13–17	Psalm **35** 1 Kings 11.26–end Acts 18.1–21
Saturday	**18 September** G	1 Timothy 6.13–16 Psalm 100 Luke 8.4–15	Psalms 41, **42**, 43 Wisdom 10.15—11.10 *or* 2 Chronicles 1.1–13 Mark 12.18–27	Psalms 45, **46** 1 Kings 12.1–24 Acts 18.22—19.7

Trinity 16

	Principal Service		3rd Service	2nd Service
Sunday 19 September 16th Sunday after Trinity — G, Proper 20	*Continuous:* Proverbs 31.10-end; Psalm 1	*Related:* Wisdom 1.16—2.1, 12-22 or Jeremiah 11.18-20; Psalm 54 — James 3.13—4.3, 7-8a; Mark 9.30-37	Psalm 119.153-176; Isaiah 45.9-22; Revelation 14.1-5	Psalm 119.137-152 [or 119.137-144]; Exodus 19.10-end; Matthew 8.23-end

	Holy Communion	3rd Service / Morning Prayer	2nd Service / Evening Prayer
Monday 20 September — Gr. John Coleridge Patteson, bishop, and companions, martyrs, 1871 (see p.83). DEL week 25	Ezra 1.1-6; Psalm 126; Luke 8.16-18	Psalm 44; Wisdom 11.21—12.2 or 2 Chronicles 2.1-16; Mark 12.28-34	Psalms 47, 49; 1 Kings 12.25—13.10; Acts 19.8-20 — *or: 1st EP of Matthew, Apostle and Evangelist:* Psalm 34; Isaiah 33.13-17; Matthew 6.19-end

	Principal Service	3rd Service	2nd Service
Tuesday 21 September — R. Matthew, Apostle and Evangelist	Proverbs 3.13-18; Psalm 119.65-72; 2 Corinthians 4.1-6; Matthew 9.9-13	MP Psalms 49, 117; 1 Kings 19.15-end; 2 Timothy 3.14-end	EP Psalm 119.33-40, 89-96; Ecclesiastes 5.4-12; Matthew 19.16-end

	Holy Communion	Morning Prayer	Evening Prayer
Wednesday 22 September — G. Ember Day	Ezra 9.5-9; Canticle: Song of Tobit or Psalm 103.1-6; Luke 9.1-6	Psalm 119.57-80; Wisdom 13.1-9 or 2 Chronicles 5; Mark 13.1-13	Psalms 59, 60 (67); 1 Kings 17; Acts 20.1-16
Thursday 23 September — G	Haggai 1.1-8; Psalm 149.1-5; Luke 9.7-9	Psalms 56, 57 (63*); Wisdom 16.15—17.1 or 2 Chronicles 6.1-21; Mark 13.14-23	Psalms 61, 62, 64; 1 Kings 18.1-20; Acts 20.17-end
Friday 24 September — G. Ember Day	Haggai 1.15b—2.9; Psalm 43; Luke 9.18-22	Psalms 51, 54; Wisdom 18.6-19 or 2 Chronicles 6.22-end; Mark 13.24-31	Psalm 38; 1 Kings 18.21-end; Acts 21.1-16
Saturday 25 September — Gw. Lancelot Andrewes, bishop, spiritual writer, 1626 (see p.85). *Sergei of Radonezh, monastic reformer, teacher of the faith, 1392.* Ember Day	Zechariah 2.1-5, 10-11; Psalm 125 or Canticle: Jeremiah 31.10-13; Luke 9.43b-45	Psalm 68; Wisdom 19 or 2 Chronicles 7; Mark 13.32-end	Psalms 65, 66; 1 Kings 19; Acts 21.17-36

Trinity 17

		Principal Service		3rd Service	2nd Service
Sunday	**26 September** G **17th Sunday after Trinity** Proper 21	*Continuous:* Esther 7.1–6, 9, 10; 9.20–22 Psalm 124	*Related:* Numbers 11.4–6, 10–16, 24–29 Psalm 19.7–end James 5.13–end Mark 9.38–end	Psalm 122 Isaiah 48.12–end Luke 11.37–end	Psalms 120, 12 Exodus 24 Matthew 9.1–8

		Holy Communion	Morning Prayer	Evening Prayer
Monday	**27 September** Gw Vincent de Paul, founder of the Lazarists, 1660 (see p.86) DEL week 26	Zechariah 8.1–8 Psalm 102.12–22 Luke 9.46–50	Psalm 71 1 Maccabees 1.1–19 or 2 Chronicles 9.1–12 Mark 14.1–11	Psalms 72, 75 1 Kings 21 Acts 21.37—22.21
Tuesday	**28 September** G	Zechariah 8.20–end Psalm 87 Luke 9.51–56	Psalm 73 1 Maccabees 1.20–40 or 2 Chronicles 10.1—11.4 Mark 14.12–25	Psalm 74 1 Kings 22.1–28 Acts 22.22—23.11 *or:* 1st EP of Michael and All Angels: Psalm 91; 2 Kings 6.8–17; Matthew 18.1–6, 10

		Principal Service	3rd Service	2nd Service
Wednesday	**29 September** W Michael and All Angels	Genesis 28.10–17 or Revelation 12.7–12 Psalm 103.19–end Revelation 12.7–12 or Hebrews 1.5–end John 1.47–end	*MP* Psalms 34, 150 Tobit 12.6–end or Daniel 12.1–4 Acts 12.1–11	*EP* Psalms 138, 148 Daniel 10.4–end Revelation 5

		Holy Communion	Morning Prayer	Evening Prayer
Thursday	**30 September** G *Jerome, translator, teacher of the faith, 420*	Nehemiah 8.1–12 Psalm 19.7–11 Luke 10.1–12	Psalm 78.1–39* 1 Maccabees 2.1–28 or 2 Chronicles 13.1—14.1 Mark 14.43–52	Psalm 78.40–end* 2 Kings 1.2–17 Acts 24.1–23
Friday	**1 October** G *Remigius, bishop, 533* *Anthony Ashley Cooper (Earl of Shaftesbury),* *social reformer, 1885*	Baruch 1.15–end or Deuteronomy 31.7–13 Psalm 79.1–9 Luke 10.13–16	Psalm 55 1 Maccabees 2.29–48 or 2 Chronicles 14.2–end Mark 14.53–65	Psalm 69 2 Kings 2.1–18 Acts 24.24—25.12
Saturday	**2 October** G	Baruch 4.5–12, 27–29 or Joshua 22.1–6 Psalm 69.33–37 Luke 10.17–24	Psalms 76, 79 1 Maccabees 2.49–end or 2 Chronicles 15.1–15 Mark 14.66–end	Psalms 81, 84 2 Kings 4.1–37 Acts 25.13–end

		Principal Service		3rd Service	2nd Service
Sunday	**3 October** G **18th Sunday after Trinity** Proper 22	*Continuous:* Job 1.1; 2.1–10 Psalm 26	*Related:* Genesis 2.18–24 Psalm 8 Hebrews 1.1–4; 2.5–12 Mark 10.2–16	Psalms 123, 124 Isaiah 49.13–23 Luke 12.1–12	Psalms 125, 126 Joshua 3.7–end Matthew 10.1–22
		Holy Communion		**Morning Prayer**	**Evening Prayer**
Monday	**4 October** Gw Francis of Assisi, friar, deacon, 1226 (see p.86) DEL week 27	Jonah 1.1—2.2, 10 Canticle: Jonah 2.2–4, 7 or Ps 69.1–6 Luke 10.25–37		Psalms 80, 82 1 Maccabees 3.1–26 or 2 Chronicles 17.1–12 Mark 15.1–15	Psalms 85, 86 2 Kings 5 Acts 26.1–23
Tuesday	**5 October** G	Jonah 3 Psalm 130 Luke 10.38–end		Psalms 87, **89**.1–18 1 Maccabees 3.27–41 or 2 Chronicles 18.1–27 Mark 15.16–32	Psalm **89**.19–end 2 Kings 6.1–23 Acts 26.24–end
Wednesday	**6 October** Gr William Tyndale, translator, martyr, 1536 (see p.83)	Jonah 4 Psalm 86.1–9 Luke 11.1–4		Psalm 119.105–128 1 Maccabees 3.42–end or 2 Chronicles 18.28—end of 19 Mark 15.33–41	Psalms 91, 93 2 Kings 9.1–16 Acts 27.1–26
Thursday	**7 October** G	Malachi 3.13—4.2a Psalm 1 Luke 11.5–13		Psalms 90, **92** 1 Maccabees 4.1–25 or 2 Chronicles 20.1–23 Mark 15.42–end	Psalm **94** 2 Kings 9.17–end Acts 27.27–end
Friday	**8 October** G	Joel 1.13–15, 2.1–2 Psalm 9.1–7 Luke 11.15–26		Psalms **88** (95) 1 Maccabees 4.26–35 or 2 Chronicles 22.10—end of 23 Mark 16.1–8	Psalm **102** 2 Kings 12.1–19 Acts 28.1–16
Saturday	**9 October** G *Denys, bishop, and companions, martyrs, c.250* *Robert Grosseteste, bishop, philosopher, scientist, 1253*	Joel 3.12–end Psalm 97.1, 8–end Luke 11.27–28		Psalms 96, **97**, 100 1 Maccabees 4.36–end or 2 Chronicles 24.1–22 Mark 16.9–end	Psalm **104** 2 Kings 17.1–23 Acts 28.17–end

Trinity 19

Day		Principal Service	3rd Service	2nd Service
Sunday	**10 October** G **19th Sunday after Trinity** Proper 23	*Continuous:* Job 23.1–9, 16–end Psalm 22.1–15 *Related:* Amos 5.6–7, 10–15 Psalm 90.12–end Hebrews 4.12–end Mark 10.17–31	Psalms 129, 130 Isaiah 50.4–10 Luke 13.22–30	Psalms 127 [128] Joshua 5.13—6.20 Matthew 11.20–30

		Holy Communion	**Morning Prayer**	**Evening Prayer**
Monday	**11 October** G *Ethelburga, abbess, 675* *James the Deacon,* *companion of Paulinus, 7th cent.* DEL week 28	Romans 1.1–7 Psalm 98 Luke 11.29–32	Psalms 98, 99, 101 1 Maccabees 6.1–17 or 2 Chronicles 26.1–21 John 13.1–11	Psalm 105* (or 103) 2 Kings 17.24–end Philippians 1.1–11
Tuesday	**12 October** Gw *Wilfrid, bishop, missionary, 709 (see p.86)* *Elizabeth Fry, prison reformer, 1845* *Edith Cavell, nurse, 1915*	Romans 1.16–25 Psalm 19.1–4 Luke 11.37–41	Psalm 106* (or 103) 1 Maccabees 6.18–47 or 2 Chronicles 28 John 13.12–20	Psalm 107* 2 Kings 18.1–12 Philippians 1.12–end
Wednesday	**13 October** Gw *Edward the Confessor, king, 1066* (see p.87)	Romans 2.1–11 Psalm 62.1–8 Luke 11.42–46	Psalms 110, 111, 112 1 Maccabees 7.1–20 or 2 Chronicles 29.1–19 John 13.21–30	Psalm 119.129–152 2 Kings 18.13–end Philippians 2.1–13
Thursday	**14 October** G	Romans 3.21–30 Psalm 130 Luke 11.47–end	Psalms 113, 115 1 Maccabees 7.21–end or 2 Chronicles 29.20–end John 13.31–end	Psalms 114, 116, 117 2 Kings 19.1–19 Philippians 2.14–end
Friday	**15 October** Gw *Teresa of Avila, teacher of the faith, 1582* (see p.84)	Romans 4.1–8 Psalm 32 Luke 12.1–7	Psalm 139 1 Maccabees 9.1–22 or 2 Chronicles 30 John 14.1–14	Psalms 130, 131, 137 2 Kings 19.20–36 Philippians 3.1—4.1
Saturday	**16 October** G *Nicholas Ridley and Hugh Latimer, bishops,* *martyrs, 1555*	Romans 4.13, 16–18 Psalm 105.6–10, 41–44 Luke 12.8–12	Psalms 120, 121, 122 1 Maccabees 13.41–end, 14.4–15 or 2 Chronicles 32.1–22 John 14.15–end	Psalm 118 2 Kings 20 Philippians 4.2–end

			Principal Service	3rd Service	2nd Service
Sunday	**17 October** **20th Sunday after Trinity** Proper 24	G	*Continuous:* Job 38.1–7 [34–end] Psalm 104.1–10, 26, 35c [or 104.1–10] *Related:* Isaiah 53.4–end Psalm 91.9–end Hebrews 5.1–10 Mark 10.35–45	Psalms 133, 134, 137.1–6 Isaiah 54.1–14 Luke 13.31–end	Psalm 141 Joshua 14.6–14 Matthew 12.1–21 *or:* 1st EP of Luke the Evangelist: Psalm 33; Hosea 6.1–3; 2 Timothy 3.10–end
Monday	**18 October** Luke the Evangelist	R	Isaiah 35.3–6 or Acts 16.6–12a Psalm 147.1–7 2 Timothy 4.5–17 Luke 10.1–9	*MP* Psalms 145, 146 Isaiah 55 Luke 1.1–4	*EP* Psalm 103 Ecclesiasticus 38.1–14 or Isaiah 61.1–6 Colossians 4.7–end
			Holy Communion	**Morning Prayer**	**Evening Prayer**
Tuesday	**19 October** Henry Martyn, translator, missionary, 1812 (see p.86) DEL week 29	Gw	Romans 5.12, 15, 17–end Psalm 40.7–12 Luke 12.35–38	Psalms 132, 133 2 Maccabees 6.12–end or 2 Chronicles 34.1–18 John 15.12–17	Psalms (134) 135 2 Kings 22.1–23.3 1 Timothy 1.18–end of 2
Wednesday	**20 October**	G	Romans 6.12–18 Psalm 124 Luke 12.39–48	Psalm 119.153–end 2 Maccabees 7.1–19 or 2 Chronicles 34.19–end John 15.18–end	Psalm 136 2 Kings 23.4–25 1 Timothy 3
Thursday	**21 October**	G	Romans 6.19–end Psalm 1 Luke 12.49–53	Psalms 143, 146 2 Maccabees 7.20–41 or 2 Chronicles 35.1–19 John 16.1–15	Psalms 138, 140, 141 2 Kings 23.36–24.17 1 Timothy 4
Friday	**22 October**	G	Romans 7.18–end Psalm 119.33–40 Luke 12.54–end	Psalms 142, 144 Tobit 1 or 2 Chronicles 35.20–36.10 John 16.16–22	Psalm 145 2 Kings 24.18–25.12 1 Timothy 5.1–16
Saturday	**23 October**	G	Romans 8.1–11 Psalm 24.1–6 Luke 13.1–9	Psalm 147 Tobit 2 or 2 Chronicles 36.11–end John 16.23–end	Psalms 148, 149, 150 2 Kings 25.22–end 1 Timothy 5.17–end

Last after Trinity

	Principal Service	3rd Service	2nd Service
Sunday **24 October** **Last Sunday after Trinity** Proper 25 G	*Continuous:* Job 42.1–6, 10–end Psalm 34.1–8, 19–end [or 34.1–8] *Related:* Jeremiah 31.7–9 Psalm 126 Hebrews 7.23–end Mark 10.46–end	Psalm 119.89–104 Isaiah 59.9–20 Luke 14.1–14	Psalm 119.121–136 Ecclesiastes 11, 12 2 Timothy 2.1–7 HC Luke 18.9–14
or Sunday **24 October** **Bible Sunday** G	Isaiah 55.1–11 Psalm 19.7–end 2 Timothy 3.14–4.5 John 5.36b–end	Psalm 119.89–104 Isaiah 45.22–end Matthew 24.30–35 or Luke 14.1–14	Psalm 119.1–16 2 Kings 22 Colossians 3.12–17 HC Luke 4.14–30

or, if the date of dedication of a church is not known, the Dedication Festival (Gold or W) may be celebrated today or on 3 October, or on a suitable date chosen locally (see p.82)

	Holy Communion	Morning Prayer	Evening Prayer
Monday **25 October** *Crispin and Crispinian, martyrs, c.287* DEL week 30 G	Romans 8.12–17 Psalm 68.1–6, 19 Luke 13.10–17	Psalms 1, 2, 3 Tobit 3 or Micah 1.1–9 John 17.1–5	Psalms 4, 7 Judith 4 or Exodus 22.21–27, 23.1–17 1 Timothy 6.1–10
Tuesday **26 October** *Alfred, king, scholar, 899 (see p.87)* *Cedd, abbot, bishop, 664* Gw	Romans 8.18–25 Psalm 126 Luke 13.18–21	Psalms 5, 6 (8) Tobit 4 or Micah 2 John 17.6–19	Psalms 9, 10* Judith 5.1–6.4 or Exodus 29.38–30.16 1 Timothy 6.11–end
Wednesday **27 October** G	Romans 8.26–30 Psalm 13 Luke 13.22–30	Psalm 119.1–32 Tobit 5.1–6.1a or Micah 3 John 17.20–end	Psalms 11, 12, 13 Judith 6.10—7.7 or Leviticus 8 2 Timothy 1.1–14 *or:* 1st EP of Simon and Jude, Apostles: Psalms 124, 125, 126; Deuteronomy 32.1–4; John 14.15–26

	Principal Service	3rd Service	2nd Service
Thursday **28 October** Simon and Jude, Apostles R	Isaiah 28.14–16 Psalm 119.89–96 Ephesians 2.19–end John 15.17–end	MP Psalms 116, 117 Wisdom 5.1–16 or Isaiah 45.18–end Luke 6.12–16	EP Psalm 119.1–16 1 Maccabees 2.42–66 or Jeremiah 3.11–18 Jude 1–4, 17–end

	Holy Communion	Morning Prayer	Evening Prayer
Friday **29 October** *James Hannington, bishop, martyr,* *1885 (see p.83)* Gr	Romans 9.1–5 Psalm 147.13–end Luke 14.1–6	Psalms 17, 19 Tobit 7 or Micah 5.2–end John 18.12–27	Psalm 22 Judith 8.9–end or Leviticus 16.2–24 2 Timothy 2.14–end

4 before Advent / All Saints' Day

All Saints' Day is celebrated either on Monday 1 November or on Sunday 31 October; if the latter, there may be a supplementary celebration on 1 November.

If All Saints' Day is celebrated on Monday 1 November only:

		Holy Communion	Morning Prayer	Evening Prayer
Saturday	**30 October** G	Romans 11.1–2, 11–12, 25–29 Psalm 94.14–19 Luke 14.1, 7–11	Psalms 20, 21, **23** Tobit 8 or Micah 6 John 18.28–end	Psalms **24**, 25 Judith 9 or Leviticus 17 2 Timothy 3
		Principal Service	**3rd Service**	**2nd Service**
Sunday	**31 October** *R/G* **4th Sunday before Advent**	Deuteronomy 6.1–9 Psalm 119.1–8 Hebrews 9.11–14 Mark 12.28–34	Psalms 112, 149 Jeremiah 31.31–34 1 John 3.1–3	**1st EP of All Saints' Day** Psalms 1, 5 Ecclesiasticus 44.1–15 or Isaiah 40.27–end Revelation 19.6–10
Monday	**1 November** *Gold or W* **All Saints' Day**	Wisdom 3.1–9 or Isaiah 25.6–9 Psalm 24.1–6 Revelation 21.1–6a John 11.32–44	MP Psalms 15, 84, 149 Isaiah 35.1–9 Luke 9.18–27	EP Psalms 148, 150 Isaiah 65.17–end Hebrews 11.32—12.2

4 before Advent / All Saints' Day

If All Saints' Day is celebrated on Sunday 31 October only:

		Holy Communion	Morning Prayer	Evening Prayer
Saturday 30 October	G	Romans 11.1–2, 11–12, 25–29 Psalm 94.14–19 Luke 14.1, 7–11	Psalms 20, 21, **23** Tobit 8 or Micah 6 John 18.28–end	**1st EP of All Saints' Day** Psalms 1, 5 Ecclesiasticus 44.1–15 or Isaiah 40.27–end Revelation 19.6–10
		Principal Service	*3rd Service*	*2nd Service*
Sunday 31 October All Saints' Day	*Gold or W*	Wisdom 3.1–9 or Isaiah 25.6–9 Psalm 24.1–6 Revelation 21.1–6a John 11.32–44	MP Psalms 15, 84, 149 Isaiah 35.1–9 Luke 9.18–27	EP Psalms 148, 150 Isaiah 65.17–end Hebrews 11.32—12.2
		Holy Communion	*Morning Prayer*	*Evening Prayer*
Monday 1 November DEL week 31	*R/G*	Romans 11.29–end Psalm 69.31–37 Luke 14.12–14	Psalms **2**, 146 or 27, **30** Isaiah 1.1–20 Matthew 1.18–end	Psalms **92**, 96, 97 or 26, **28**, 29 Daniel 1 Revelation 1

Or, if All Saints' Day is celebrated on Monday 1 November in addition to Sunday 31 October:

		Principal Service	3rd Service	2nd Service
Monday 1 November All Saints' Day	*Gold or W*	Isaiah 56.3–8 or 2 Esdras 2.42–end Psalm 33.1–5 Hebrews 12.18–24 Matthew 5.1–12	MP Psalms 111, 112, 117 Wisdom 5.1–16 or Jeremiah 31.31–34 2 Corinthians 4.5–12	EP Psalm 145 Isaiah 66.20–23 Colossians 1.9–14

4 before Advent

	Holy Communion	Morning Prayer	Evening Prayer
Tuesday Rp/Gp **2 November** Commemoration of the Faithful Departed (All Souls' Day) DEL week 31	Romans 12.5–16 Psalm 131 Luke 14.15–24 *Lesser Festival eucharistic lectionary:* Lamentations 3.17–26, 31–33 or Wisdom 3.1–9 Psalm 23 or 27.1–6,16–end Romans 5.5–11 or 1 Peter 1.3–9 John 5.19–25 or John 6.37–40	Psalms **5**, 147.1–12 or 32, **36** Isaiah 1.21–end Matthew 2.1–15	Psalms 98, 99, **100** or **33** Daniel 2.1–24 Revelation 2.1–11
Wednesday Rw/Gw **3 November** Richard Hooker, priest, teacher of the faith, 1600 (see p.84) *Martin of Porres, friar, 1639*	Romans 13.8–10 Psalm 112 Luke 14.25–33	Psalms **9**, 147.13–end or **34** Isaiah 2.1–11 Matthew 2.16–end	Psalm 111, **112**, 116 or 119.**33–56** Daniel 2.25–end Revelation 2.12–end
Thursday R/G **4 November**	Romans 14.7–12 Psalm 27.14–end Luke 15.1–10	Psalms 11, **15**, 148 or **37*** Isaiah 2.12–end Matthew 3	Psalm 118 or 39, **40** Daniel 3.1–18 Revelation 3.1–13
Friday R/G **5 November**	Romans 15.14–21 Psalm 98 Luke 16.1–8	Psalms **16**, 149 or **31** Isaiah 3.1–15 Matthew 4.1–11	Psalms 137, 138, **143** or **35** Daniel 3.19–end Revelation 3.14–end
Saturday R/G **6 November** *Leonard, hermit, 6th cent.* William Temple, archbishop, teacher of the faith, 1944	Romans 16.3–9, 16, 22–end Psalm 145.1–7 Luke 16.9–15	Psalms 18.**31–end**, 150 or 41, **42, 43** Isaiah 4.2—5.7 Matthew 4.12–22	Psalm 145 or 45, **46** Daniel 4.1–18 Revelation 4

	Principal Service	3rd Service	2nd Service
	Holy Communion	Morning Prayer	Evening Prayer
Sunday *R/G* **7 November** **3rd Sunday before Advent**	Jonah 3.1–5, 10 Psalm 62.5–end Hebrews 9.24–end Mark 1.14–20	Psalm 136 Micah 4.1–5 Philippians 4.6–9	Psalms 46 [82] Isaiah 10.33—11.9 John 14.1–29 (or 23–29)
Monday *Rw/Gw* **8 November** Saints and martyrs of England DEL week 32	Wisdom 1.1–7 *or* Titus 1.1–9 Psalm139.1–9 *or* 24.1–6 Luke 17.1–6 *Lesser Festival eucharistic lectionary:* Isaiah 61.4–9 *or* Ecclesiasticus 44.1–15 Psalm 15 Revelation 19.5–10 John 17.18–23	Psalms 19, **20** *or* **44** Isaiah 5.8–24 Matthew 4.23—5.12	Psalm **34** *or* 47, **49** Daniel 4.19–end Revelation 5
Tuesday *R/G* **9 November** *Margery Kempe, mystic, c.1440*	Wisdom 2.23—3.9 *or* Titus 2.1–8, 11–14 Psalm 34.1–6 *or* 37.3–5, 30–32 Luke 17.7–10	Psalms 21, 24 *or* **48**, 52 Isaiah 5.25–end Matthew 5.13–20	Psalms 36, **40** *or* **50** Daniel 5.1–12 Revelation 6
Wednesday *Rw/Gw* **10 November** Leo the Great, bishop, teacher of the faith, 461 (see p.84)	Wisdom 6.1–11 *or* Titus 3.1–7 Psalm 82 *or* 23 Luke 17.11–19	Psalms 23, 25 *or* 11**9.57–80** Isaiah 6 Matthew 5.21–37	Psalm **37** *or* **59**, 60 (67) Daniel 5.13–end Revelation 7.1–4, 9–end
Thursday *Rw/Gw* **11 November** Martin, bishop, c.397 (see p.85)	Wisdom 7.22—8.1 *or* Philemon 7–20 Psalm 119.89–96 *or* 146.4–end Luke 17.20–25	Psalms **26**, 27 *or* 56, **57** (63*) Isaiah 7.1–17 Matthew 5.38–end	Psalms 42, **43** *or* 61, **62**, 64 Daniel 6 Revelation 8
Friday *R/G* **12 November**	Wisdom 13.1–9 *or* 2 John 4–9 Psalm 19.1–4 *or* 119.1–8 Luke 17.26–end	Psalms 28, **32** *or* **51**, 54 Isaiah 8.1–15 Matthew 6.1–18	Psalm **31** *or* **38** Daniel 7.1–14 Revelation 9.1–12
Saturday *Rw/Gw* **13 November** Charles Simeon, priest, evangelical divine, 1836 (see p.85)	Wisdom 18.14–16, 19.6–9 *or* 3 John 5–8 Psalm 105.1–5, 35–42 *or* 112 Luke 18.1–8	Psalm **33** *or* **68** Isaiah 8.16—9.7 Matthew 6.19–end	Psalms 84, **86** *or* 65, **66** Daniel 7.15–end Revelation 9.13–end

2 before Advent

		Principal Service	3rd Service	2nd Service
Sunday	**14 November** R/G **2nd Sunday before Advent** *Remembrance Sunday*	Daniel 12.1–3 Psalm 16 Hebrews 10.11–14 [15–18] 19–25 Mark 13.1–8	Psalm 96 1 Samuel 9.27—10.2*a*; 10.17–26 Matthew 13.31–35	Psalm 95 Daniel 3 [or 3.13–end] Matthew 13.24–30, 36–43
		Holy Communion	**Morning Prayer**	**Evening Prayer**
Monday	**15 November** R/G DEL week 33	1 Maccabees 1.10–15, 41–43, 54–57, 62–64 or Revelation 1.1–4, 2.1–5 Psalm 79.1–5 or 1 Luke 18.35–end	Psalms 46, 47 or 71 Isaiah 9.8—10.4 Matthew 7.1–12	Psalms 70, 71 or 72, 75 Daniel 8.1–14 Revelation 10
Tuesday	**16 November** Rw/Gw Margaret, queen, philanthropist, 1093 (see p.87) *Edmund Rich, archbishop, 1240*	2 Maccabees 6.18–end or Revelation 3.1–6, 14–end Psalm 11 or 15 Luke 19.1–10	Psalms 48, 52 or 73 Isaiah 10.5–19 Matthew 7.13–end	Psalms 67, 72 or 74 Daniel 8.15–end Revelation 11.1–14
Wednesday	**17 November** Rw/Gw Hugh, bishop, 1200 (see p.85)	2 Maccabees 7.1, 20–31 or Revelation 4 Psalm 116.10–end or 150 Luke 19.11–28	Psalms 56, 57 or 77 Isaiah 10.20–32 Matthew 8.1–13	Psalm 73 or 119.81–104 Daniel 9.1–19 Revelation 11.15–end
Thursday	**18 November** Rw/Gw Elizabeth, princess, philanthropist, 1231 (see p.87)	1 Maccabees 2.15–29 or Revelation 5.1–10 Psalm 129 or 149.1–5 Luke 19.41–44	Psalms 61, 62 or 78.1–39* Isaiah 10.33—11.9 Matthew 8.14–22	Psalms 74, 76 or 78.40–end* Daniel 9.20–end Revelation 12
Friday	**19 November** Rw/Gw Hilda, abbess, 680 (see p.86) *Mechtild, béguine, mystic, 1280*	1 Maccabees 4.36–37, 52–59 or Revelation 10.8–11 Psalm 122 or 119.65–72 Luke 19.45–end	Psalms 63, 65 or 55 Isaiah 11.10—end of 12 Matthew 8.23–end	Psalm 77 or 69 Daniel 10.1—11.1 Revelation 13.1–10
Saturday	**20 November** R/Gr Edmund, king, martyr, 870 (see p.83) *Priscilla Lydia Sellon, a restorer of the religious life in the Church of England, 1876*	1 Maccabees 6.1–13 or Revelation 11.4–12 Psalm 124 or 144.1–9 Luke 20.27–40	Psalm 78.1–39 or 76, 79 Isaiah 13.1–13 Matthew 9.1–17	Psalm 78.1–40 or 81, 84 Daniel 12 Revelation 13.11–end or: 1st EP of Christ the King: Psalms 99, 100: Isaiah 10.33—11.9; 1 Timothy 6.11–16

Christ the King / Sunday next before Advent

		Principal Service	3rd Service	2nd Service
Sunday	**21 November** R/W Christ the King Sunday next before Advent	Daniel 7.9–10, 13, 14 Psalm 93 Revelation 1.4b–8 John 18.33–37	MP Psalm 29, 110 Isaiah 32.1–8 Revelation 3.7–end	EP Psalm 72 [or 72.1–7] Daniel 5 John 6.1–15
		Holy Communion	Morning Prayer	Evening Prayer
Monday	**22 November** R/G Cecilia, martyr, c.230 DEL week 34	Daniel 1.1–6, 8–20 Canticle: Bless the Lord Luke 21.1–4	Psalms 92, **96** or 80, 82 Isaiah 14.3–20 Matthew 9.18–34	Psalms 80, 81 or 85, 86 Isaiah 40.1–11 Revelation 14.1–13
Tuesday	**23 November** R/Gr Clement, bishop, martyr, c.100 (see p.83)	Daniel 2.31–45 Canticle: Benedicite 1–3 Luke 21.5–11	Psalms **97**, 98, 100 or 87, **89.1–18** Isaiah 17 Matthew 9.35—10.15	Psalms 99, **101** or **89.19–end** Isaiah 40.12–26 Revelation 14.14—end of 15
Wednesday	**24 November** R/G	Daniel 5.1–6, 13–14, 16–17, 23–28 Canticle: Benedicite 4–5 Luke 21.12–19	Psalms 110, 111, **112** or 119.**105–128** Isaiah 19 Matthew 10.16–33	Psalms 121, **122**, 123, 124 or **91**, 93 Isaiah 40.27—41.7 Revelation 16.1–11
Thursday	**25 November** R/G Catherine, martyr, 4th cent. Isaac Watts, hymn writer, 1748	Daniel 6.12–end Canticle: Benedicite 6–8a Luke 21.20–28	Psalms **125**, 126, 127, 128 or 90, **92** Isaiah 21.1–12 Matthew 10.34—11.1	Psalms 131, 132, **133** or **94** Isaiah 41.8–20 Revelation 16.12–end
Friday	**26 November** R/G	Daniel 7.2–14 Canticle: Benedicite 8b–10a Luke 21.29–33	Psalm **139** or **88** (95) Isaiah 22.1–14 Matthew 11.2–19	Psalms **146**, 147 or **102** Isaiah 41.21–42.9 Revelation 17
Saturday	**27 November** R/G	Daniel 7.15–27 Canticle: Benedicite 10b–end Luke 21.34–36	Psalms **145** or 96, **97**, 100 Isaiah 24 Matthew 11.20–end	Psalms 148, 149, **150** or **104** Isaiah 42.10–17 Revelation 18

¶ *Additional Weekday Lectionary*

This Additional Weekday Lectionary provides two readings for each day of the year, except for Sundays, Principal Feasts and other Principal Holy Days, Holy Week and Festivals (for which the readings provided in the main body of this lectionary are used). The readings for 'first evensongs' in the main body of the lectionary are used on the eves of Principal Feasts and may be used on the eves of Festivals. This lectionary is intended particularly for use in those places of worship that attract occasional rather than daily worshippers, and can be used either at Morning or Evening Prayer. Psalmody is not provided and should be taken from the daily provision earlier in this volume.

	29 November – Advent 1		
Monday	**30 November**	Andrew the Apostle – see p.10	
Tuesday	**1 December**	Zephaniah 3.14–end	1 Thessalonians 4.13–end
Wednesday	**2 December**	Isaiah 65.17—66.2	Matthew 24.1–14
Thursday	**3 December**	Micah 5.2–5a	John 3.16–21
Friday	**4 December**	Isaiah 66.18–end	Luke 13.22–30
Saturday	**5 December**	Micah 7.8–15	Romans 15.30—16.7, 25–end
	6 December – Advent 2		
Monday	**7 December**	Jeremiah 7.1–11	Philippians 4.4–9
Tuesday	**8 December**	Daniel 7.9–14	Matthew 24.15–28
Wednesday	**9 December**	Amos 9.11–end	Romans 13.8–end
Thursday	**10 December**	Jeremiah 23.5–8	Mark 11.1–11
Friday	**11 December**	Jeremiah 33.14–22	Luke 21.25–36
Saturday	**12 December**	Zechariah 14.4–11	Revelation 22.1–7
	13 December – Advent 3		
Monday	**14 December**	Isaiah 40.1–11	Matthew 3.1–12
Tuesday	**15 December**	Lamentations 3.22–33	1 Corinthians 1.1–9
Wednesday	**16 December**	Joel 3.9–16	Matthew 24.29–35
Thursday	**17 December**	Ecclesiasticus 24.1–9 or Proverbs 8.22–31	1 Corinthians 2.1–13
Friday	**18 December**	Exodus 3.1–6	Acts 7.20–36
Saturday	**19 December**	Isaiah 11.1–9	Romans 15.7–13
	20 December – Advent 4		
Monday	**21 December**	Numbers 24.15b–19	Revelation 22.10–21
Tuesday	**22 December**	Jeremiah 30.7–11a	Acts 4.1–12
Wednesday	**23 December**	Isaiah 7.10–15	Matthew 1.18–23
Thursday	**24 December**	*At Evening Prayer the readings for Christmas Eve are used.* *At other services, the following readings are used:*	
		Isaiah 29.13–18	1 John 4.7–16
Friday	**25 December**	Christmas Day – see p.13	
Saturday	**26 December**	Stephen, deacon, first martyr – see p.13	
	27 December – John, Apostle and Evangelist / Christmas 1		
Monday	**28 December**	The Holy Innocents – see p.14	
Tuesday	**29 December**	Micah 1.1–4; 2.12–13	Luke 2.1–7
Wednesday	**30 December**	Isaiah 9.2–7	John 8.12–20
Thursday	**31 December**	Ecclesiastes 3.1–13	Revelation 21.1–8
Friday	**1 January**	Naming and Circumcision of Jesus – see p.15	
Saturday	**2 January**	Isaiah 66.6–14	Matthew 12.46–50
		If, for pastoral reasons, The Epiphany *is celebrated on Sunday 3 January, the readings for the Eve of Epiphany are used at Evening Prayer.*	

Monday	4 January	Isaiah 63.7–16	Galatians 3.23—4.7
		or if, for pastoral reasons, The Epiphany *is celebrated on Sunday*	
		3 January, the following readings are used:	
		Deuteronomy 6.4–15	John 10.31–end
Tuesday	5 January	*At Evening Prayer the readings for the Eve of the Epiphany are used.*	
		At other services, the following readings are used:	
		Isaiah 12	2 Corinthians 2.12–end
		or, if, for pastoral reasons, The Epiphany *is celebrated on Sunday*	
		3 January, the following readings are used:	
		Isaiah 63.7–16	Galatians 3.23—4.7
Wednesday	6 January	The Epiphany – see p.17	
		or, if, for pastoral reasons, The Epiphany *is celebrated on Sunday*	
		3 January, the following readings are used:	
		Isaiah 12	2 Corinthians 2.12–end
Thursday	7 January	Genesis 25.19–end	Ephesians 1.1–6
Friday	8 January	Joel 2.28–end	Ephesians 1.7–14
Saturday	9 January	*At Evening Prayer the readings for the Eve of the Baptism of Christ are used.*	
		At other services, the following readings are used:	
		Proverbs 8.12–21	Ephesians 1.15–end

Monday	11 January	Isaiah 41.14–20	John 1.29–34
Tuesday	12 January	Exodus 17.1–7	Acts 8.26–end
Wednesday	13 January	Exodus 15.1–19	Colossians 2.8–15
Thursday	14 January	Zechariah 6.9–15	1 Peter 2.4–10
Friday	15 January	Isaiah 51.7–16	Galatians 6.14–18
Saturday	16 January	Leviticus 16.11–22	Hebrews 10.19–25

Monday	18 January	1 Kings 17.8–16	Mark 8.1–10
Tuesday	19 January	1 Kings 19.1–9a	Mark 1.9–15
Wednesday	20 January	1 Kings 19.9b–18	Mark 9.2–13
Thursday	21 January	Leviticus 11.1–8, 13–19, 41–45	Acts 10.9–16
Friday	22 January	Isaiah 49.8–13	Acts 10.34–43
Saturday	23 January	Genesis 35.1–15	Acts 10.44–end

Monday	25 January	Conversion of Paul – see p.21	
Tuesday	26 January	Ezekiel 20.39–44	John 17.20–end
Wednesday	27 January	Nehemiah 2.1–10	Romans 12.1–8
Thursday	28 January	Deuteronomy 26.16–end	Romans 14.1–9
Friday	29 January	Leviticus 19.9–28	Romans 15.1–7
Saturday	30 January	*If, for pastoral reasons, the* Presentation of Christ *is celebrated on*	
		Sunday 31 January the readings for the Eve of the Presentation are used	
		at Evening Prayer.	
		At other services, the following readings are used:	
		Jeremiah 33.1–11	1 Peter 5.5b–end

Monday	1 February	Jonah 3	2 Corinthians 5.11–21
		If the Presentation of Christ *is celebrated on Tuesday 2 February the*	
		readings for the Eve of the Presentation are used at Evening Prayer.	
Tuesday	2 February	Presentation of Christ – see p.22	
		or, if, for pastoral reasons, the Presentation of Christ *is celebrated on*	
		Sunday 31 January, the following readings are used:	
		Proverbs 4.10–end	Matthew 5.31–20
Wednesday	3 February	Isaiah 61.1–9	Luke 7.18–30
Thursday	4 February	Isaiah 52.1–12	Matthew 10.1–15
Friday	5 February	Isaiah 56.1–8	Matthew 28.16–end
Saturday	6 February	Habakkuk 2.1–4	Revelation 14.1–7

Monday	8 February	Isaiah 61.1–9	Mark 6.1–13
Tuesday	9 February	Isaiah 52.1–10	Romans 10.5–21
Wednesday	10 February	Isaiah 52.13—53.6	Romans 15.14–21
Thursday	11 February	Isaiah 53.4–12	2 Corinthians 4.1–10
Friday	12 February	Zechariah 8.16–end	Matthew 10.1–15
Saturday	13 February	Jeremiah 1.4–10	Matthew 10.16–22

14 February – Next before Lent

Monday	15 February	2 Kings 2.13–22	3 John
Tuesday	16 February	Judges 14.5–17	Revelation 10.4–11
Wednesday	17 February	Ash Wednesday – see p.26	
Thursday	18 February	Genesis 2.7–end	Hebrews 2.5–end
Friday	19 February	Genesis 4.1–12	Hebrews 4.12–end
Saturday	20 February	2 Kings 22.11–end	Hebrews 5.1–10

21 February – Lent 1

Monday	22 February	Genesis 6.11–end, 7.11–16	Luke 4.14–21
Tuesday	23 February	Deuteronomy 31.7–13	1 John 3.1–10
Wednesday	24 February	Genesis 11.1–9	Matthew 24.15–28
Thursday	25 February	Genesis 13.1–13	1 Peter 2.13–end
Friday	26 February	Genesis 21.1–8	Luke 9.18–27
Saturday	27 February	Genesis 32.22–32	2 Peter 1.10–end

28 February – Lent 2

Monday	1 March	1 Chronicles 21.1–17	1 John 2.1–8
Tuesday	2 March	Zechariah 3	2 Peter 2.1–10a
Wednesday	3 March	Job 1.1–22	Luke 21.34—22.6
Thursday	4 March	2 Chronicles 29.1–11	Mark 11.15–19
Friday	5 March	Exodus 19.1–9a	1 Peter 1.1–9
Saturday	6 March	Exodus 19.9b–19	Acts 7.44–50

7 March – Lent 3

Monday	8 March	Joshua 4.1–13	Luke 9.1–11
Tuesday	9 March	Exodus 15.22–27	Hebrews 10.32–end
Wednesday	10 March	Genesis 9.8–17	1 Peter 3.18–end
Thursday	11 March	Daniel 12.5–end	Mark 13.21–end
Friday	12 March	Numbers 20.1–13	1 Corinthians 10.23–end
Saturday	13 March	Isaiah 43.14–end	Hebrews 3.1–15

14 March – Lent 4

Monday	15 March	2 Kings 24.18—25.7	1 Corinthians 15.20–34
Tuesday	16 March	Jeremiah 13.12–19	Acts 13.26–35
Wednesday	17 March	Jeremiah 13.20–27	1 Peter 1.17—2.3
Thursday	18 March	Jeremiah 22.11–19	Luke 11.37–52
		or 1st EP of Joseph of Nazareth	
Friday	19 March	Joseph of Nazareth – see p.30	
Saturday	20 March	Ezra 1	2 Corinthians 1.12–19

21 March – Lent 5

Monday	22 March	Joel 2.12–17	2 John
Tuesday	23 March	Isaiah 58.1–14	Mark 10.32–45
Wednesday	24 March	At Evening Prayer the readings for the Eve of the Annunciation are used. At other services, the following readings are used:	
		Job 36.1–12	John 14.1–14
Thursday	25 March	Annunciation of Our Lord to the Blessed Virgin Mary – see p.31	
Friday	26 March	Lamentations 5.1–3, 19–22	John 12.20–26
Saturday	27 March	Job 17.6–end	John 12.27–36

From the Monday of Holy Week until Easter Eve the seasonal lectionary is used: see pp.32–33.

Monday	5 April	Isaiah 54.1–14	Romans 1.1–7
Tuesday	6 April	Isaiah 51.1–11	John 5.19–29
Wednesday	7 April	Isaiah 26.1–19	John 20.1–10
Thursday	8 April	Isaiah 43.14–21	Revelation 1.4–end
Friday	9 April	Isaiah 42.10–17	I Thessalonians 5.1–11
Saturday	10 April	Job 14.1–14	John 21.1–14

11 April – Easter 2

Monday	12 April	Ezekiel 1.22–end	Revelation 4
Tuesday	13 April	Proverbs 8.1–11	Acts 16.6–15
Wednesday	14 April	Hosea 5.15—6.6	I Corinthians 15.1–11
Thursday	15 April	Jonah 2	Mark 4.35–end
Friday	16 April	Genesis 6.9–end	I Peter 3.8–end
Saturday	17 April	I Samuel 2.1–8	Matthew 28.8–15

18 April – Easter 3

Monday	19 April	Exodus 24.1–11	Revelation 5
Tuesday	20 April	Leviticus 19.9–18, 32–end	Matthew 5.38–end
Wednesday	21 April	Genesis 3.8–21	I Corinthians 15.12–28
Thursday	22 April	Isaiah 33.13–22	Mark 6.47–end
		or 1st EP of George	
Friday	23 April	George, Martyr, patron of England – see p.36	
Saturday	24 April	Isaiah 61.10—62.5	Luke 24.1–12

25 April – Easter 4

Monday	26 April	Mark the Evangelist – see p.37	
Tuesday	27 April	Job 31.13–23	Matthew 7.1–12
Wednesday	28 April	Genesis 2.4b–9	I Corinthians 15.35–49
Thursday	29 April	Proverbs 28.3–end	Mark 10.17–31
Friday	30 April	Ecclesiastes 12.1–8	Romans 6.1–11
		or 1st EP of Philip and James	
Saturday	1 May	Philip and James, Apostles – see p.37	

2 May – Easter 5

Monday	3 May	Genesis 15.1–18	Romans 4.13–end
Tuesday	4 May	Deuteronomy 8.1–10	Matthew 6.19–end
Wednesday	5 May	Hosea 13.4–14	I Corinthians 15.50–end
Thursday	6 May	Exodus 3.1–15	Mark 12.18–27
Friday	7 May	Ezekiel 36.33–end	Romans 8.1–11
Saturday	8 May	Isaiah 38.9–20	Luke 24.33–end

9 May – Easter 6

Monday	10 May	Proverbs 4.1–13	Philippians 2.1–11
Tuesday	11 May	Isaiah 32.12–end	Romans 5.1–11
Wednesday	12 May	At Evening Prayer the readings for the Eve of Ascension Day are used.	
		At other services, the following readings are used:	
		Isaiah 43.1–13	Titus 2.11—3.8
Thursday	13 May	Ascension Day – see p.39	
Friday	14 May	Matthias the Apostle – see p.39	
Saturday	15 May	Numbers 11.16–17, 24–29	I Corinthians 2

16 May – Easter 7

Monday	17 May	Numbers 27.15–end	I Corinthians 3
Tuesday	18 May	I Samuel 10.1–10	I Corinthians 12.1–13
Wednesday	19 May	I Kings 19.1–18	Matthew 3.13–end
Thursday	20 May	Ezekiel 11.14–20	Matthew 9.35—10.20
Friday	21 May	Ezekiel 36.22–28	Matthew 12.22–32
Saturday	22 May	At Evening Prayer the readings for the Eve of Pentecost are used.	
		At other services, the following readings are used:	
		Micah 3.1–8	Ephesians 6.10–20

Monday	**24 May**	Genesis 12.1–9	Romans 4.13–end
Tuesday	**25 May**	Genesis 13.1–12	Romans 12.9–end
Wednesday	**26 May**	Genesis 15	Romans 4.1–8
Thursday	**27 May**	Genesis 22.1–18	Hebrews 11.8–19
Friday	**28 May**	Isaiah 51.1–8	John 8.48–end
Saturday	**29 May**	*At Evening Prayer the readings for the Eve of Trinity Sunday are used.*	
		At other services, the following readings are used:	
		Ecclesiasticus 44.19–23	James 2.14–26
		or Joshua 2.1–15	

Monday	**31 May**	The Visit of the Blessed Virgin Mary to Elizabeth – see p.42	
Tuesday	**1 June**	Exodus 2.11–end	Acts 7.17–29
Wednesday	**2 June**	Exodus 3.1–12	Acts 7.30–38
		or 1st EP of Corpus Christi	
Thursday	**3 June**	Day of Thanksgiving for the Institution of the Holy Communion (Corpus Christi) – see p.42	
		or, where Corpus Christi is not celebrated as a Festival:	
		Exodus 6.1–13	John 9.24–38
Friday	**4 June**	Exodus 34.1–10	Mark 7.1–13
Saturday	**5 June**	Exodus 34.27–end	2 Corinthians 3.7–end

Monday	**7 June**	Genesis 37.1–11	Romans 12.9–21
Tuesday	**8 June**	Genesis 41.15–40	Mark 13.1–13
Wednesday	**9 June**	Genesis 42.17–end	Matthew 18.1–14
Thursday	**10 June**	Genesis 45.1–15	Acts 7.9–16
		or 1st EP of Barnabas	
Friday	**11 June**	Barnabas the Apostle – see p.44	
Saturday	**12 June**	Genesis 50.4–21	Luke 15.11–end

Monday	**14 June**	Isaiah 32	James 3.13–end
Tuesday	**15 June**	Proverbs 3.1–18	Matthew 5.1–12
Wednesday	**16 June**	Judges 6.1–16	Matthew 5.13–24
Thursday	**17 June**	Jeremiah 6.9–15	1 Timothy 2.1–6
Friday	**18 June**	1 Samuel 16.14–end	John 14.15–end
Saturday	**19 June**	Isaiah 6.1–9	Revelation 19.9–end

Monday	**21 June**	Exodus 13.13b–end	Luke 15.1–10
Tuesday	**22 June**	Proverbs 1.20–end	James 5.13–end
Wednesday	**23 June**	Isaiah 5.8–24	James 1.17–25
		or 1st EP of Birth of John the Baptist	
Thursday	**24 June**	Birth of John the Baptist – see p.46	
Friday	**25 June**	Jeremiah 15.15–end	Luke 16.19–31
Saturday	**26 June**	Isaiah 25.1–9	Acts 2.22–33

Monday	**28 June**	Exodus 20.1–17	Matthew 6.1–15
		or 1st EP of Peter and Paul, Apostles (or Peter the Apostle)	
Tuesday	**29 June**	Peter and Paul, Apostles or Peter the Apostle – see p.47	
Wednesday	**30 June**	Isaiah 24.1–15	1 Corinthians 6.1–11
Thursday	**1 July**	Job 7	Matthew 7.21–29
Friday	**2 July**	Jeremiah 20.7–end	Matthew 27.27–44
		or 1st EP of Thomas the Apostle	
Saturday	**3 July**	Thomas the Apostle – see p.48	

Monday	5 July	Exodus 32.1–14	Colossians 3.1–11
Tuesday	6 July	Proverbs 9.1–12	2 Thessalonians 2.13—3.5
Wednesday	7 July	Isaiah 26.1–9	Romans 8.12–27
Thursday	8 July	Jeremiah 8.18—9.6	John 13.21–35
Friday	9 July	2 Samuel 5.1–12	Matthew 27.45–56
Saturday	10 July	Hosea 11.1–11	Matthew 28.1–7

Monday	12 July	Exodus 40.1–16	Luke 14.15–24
Tuesday	13 July	Proverbs 11.1–12	Mark 12.38–44
Wednesday	14 July	Isaiah 33.2–10	Philippians 1.1–11
Thursday	15 July	Job 38	Luke 18.1–14
Friday	16 July	Job 42.1–6	John 3.1–15
Saturday	17 July	Ecclesiastes 9.1–11	Hebrews 1.1–9

Monday	19 July	Numbers 23.1–12	1 Corinthians 1.10–17
Tuesday	20 July	Proverbs 12.1–12	Galatians 3.1–14
Wednesday	21 July	Isaiah 49.8–13 or 1st EP of Mary Magdalene	2 Corinthians 8.1–11
Thursday	22 July	Mary Magdalene – see p.51	
Friday	23 July	2 Samuel 18.18–end	Matthew 27.57–66
Saturday	24 July	Isaiah 55.1–7 or 1st EP of James the Apostle	Mark 16.1–8

Monday	26 July	Joel 3.16–21	Mark 4.21–34
Tuesday	27 July	Proverbs 12.13–end	John 1.43–51
Wednesday	28 July	Isaiah 55.8–end	2 Timothy 2.8–19
Thursday	29 July	Isaiah 38.1–8	Mark 5.21–43
Friday	30 July	Jeremiah 14.1–9	Luke 8.4–15
Saturday	31 July	Ecclesiastes 5.10–19	1 Timothy 6.6–16

Monday	2 August	Joshua 1.1–9	1 Corinthians 9.19–end
Tuesday	3 August	Proverbs 15.1–11	Galatians 2.15–end
Wednesday	4 August	Isaiah 49.1–7	1 John 1
Thursday	5 August	Proverbs 27.1–12 or 1st EP of The Transfiguration	John 15.12–27
Friday	6 August	The Transfiguration of Our Lord – see p.54	
Saturday	7 August	Zechariah 7.8—8.8	Luke 20.27–40

Monday	9 August	Judges 13.1–23	Luke 10.38–42
Tuesday	10 August	Proverbs 15.15–end	Matthew 15.21–28
Wednesday	11 August	Isaiah 45.1–7	Ephesians 4.1–16
Thursday	12 August	Jeremiah 16.1–15	Luke 12.35–48
Friday	13 August	Jeremiah 18.1–11	Hebrews 1.1–9
Saturday	14 August	Jeremiah 26.1–19 or 1st EP of the Blessed Virgin Mary	Ephesians 3.1–13

Monday	16 August	Ruth 2.1–13	Luke 10.25–37
Tuesday	17 August	Proverbs 16.1–11	Philippians 3.4b–end
Wednesday	18 August	Deuteronomy 11.1–21	2 Corinthians 9.6–end
Thursday	19 August	Ecclesiasticus 2 or Ecclesiastes 2.12–25	John 16.1–15
Friday	20 August	Obadiah 1–10	John 19.1–16
Saturday	21 August	2 Kings 2.11–14	Luke 24.36–end

Monday	23 August	I Samuel 17.32–50	Matthew 8.14–22
		or 1st EP of Bartholomew the Apostle	
Tuesday	24 August	Bartholomew the Apostle – see p.58	
Wednesday	25 August	Jeremiah 5.20–end	2 Peter 3.8–end
Thursday	26 August	Daniel 2.1–23	Luke 10.1–20
Friday	27 August	Daniel 3.1–28	Revelation 15
Saturday	28 August	Daniel 6	Philippians 2.14–24

Monday	30 August	2 Samuel 7.4–17	2 Corinthians 5.1–10
Tuesday	31 August	Proverbs 18.10–21	Romans 14.10–end
Wednesday	1 September	Judges 4.1–10	Romans 1.8–17
Thursday	2 September	Isaiah 49.14–end	John 16.16–24
Friday	3 September	Job 9.1–24	Mark 15.21–32
Saturday	4 September	Exodus 19.1–9	John 20.11–18

Monday	6 September	Haggai 1	Mark 7.9–23
Tuesday	7 September	Proverbs 21.1–18	Mark 6.30–44
Wednesday	8 September	Hosea 11.1–11	1 John 4.9–end
Thursday	9 September	Lamentations 3.34–48	Romans 7.14–end
Friday	10 September	1 Kings 19.4–18	1 Thessalonians 3
Saturday	11 September	Ecclesiasticus 4.11–28	2 Timothy 3.10–end
		or Deuteronomy 29.2–15	

Monday	13 September	Wisdom 6.12–21 or Job 12.1–16	Matthew 15.1–9
		or 1st EP of Holy Cross Day	
Tuesday	14 September	Holy Cross Day – see p.61	
Wednesday	15 September	Proverbs 2.1–15	Colossians 1.9–20
Thursday	16 September	Baruch 3.14–end or Genesis 1.1–13	John 1.1–18
Friday	17 September	Ecclesiasticus 1.1–20	1 Corinthians 1.18–end
		or Deuteronomy 7.7–16	
Saturday	18 September	Wisdom 9.1–12	Luke 2.41–end
		or Jeremiah 1.4–10	

Monday	20 September	Genesis 21.1–13	Luke 1.26–38
		or 1st EP of Matthew, Apostle and Evangelist	
Tuesday	21 September	Matthew, Apostle and Evangelist – see p.62	
Wednesday	22 September	2 Kings 4.1–7	John 2.1–11
Thursday	23 September	2 Kings 4.25b–37	Mark 3.19b–35
Friday	24 September	Judith 8.9–17, 28–36 or Ruth 1.1–18	John 19.25b–30
Saturday	25 September	Exodus 15.19–27	Acts 1.6–14

Monday	27 September	Exodus 19.16–end	Hebrews 12.18–end
Tuesday	28 September	1 Chronicles 16.1–13	Revelation 11.15–end
		or 1st EP of Michael and All Angels	
Wednesday	29 September	Michael and All Angels – see p.63	
Thursday	30 September	Nehemiah 8.1–12	1 Corinthians 14.1–12
Friday	1 October	Isaiah 1.10–17	Mark 12.28–34
Saturday	2 October	Daniel 6.6–23	Revelation 12.7–12

Monday	4 October	2 Samuel 22.4–7, 17–20	Hebrews 7.26—8.6
Tuesday	5 October	Proverbs 22.17–end	2 Corinthians 12.1–10
Wednesday	6 October	Hosea 14	James 2.14–26
Thursday	7 October	Isaiah 24.1–15	John 16.25–33
Friday	8 October	Jeremiah 14.1–9	Luke 23.44–56
Saturday	9 October	Zechariah 8.14–end	John 20.19–end

Monday	**11 October**	I Kings 3.3–14	I Timothy 3.14—4.8
Tuesday	**12 October**	Proverbs 27.11–end	Galatians 6.1–10
Wednesday	**13 October**	Isaiah 51.1–6	2 Corinthians 1.1–11
Thursday	**14 October**	Ecclesiasticus 18.1–14 *or* Job 26	I Corinthians 11.17–end
Friday	**15 October**	Ecclesiasticus 28.2–12	Mark 15.33–47
		or Job 19.21–end	
Saturday	**16 October**	Isaiah 44.21–end	John 21.15–end

Monday	**18 October**	Luke the Evangelist – see p.66	
Tuesday	**19 October**	Proverbs 31.10–end	Luke 10.38–42
Wednesday	**20 October**	Jonah 1	Luke 5.1–11
Thursday	**21 October**	Exodus 12.1–20	I Thessalonians 4.1–12
Friday	**22 October**	Isaiah 64	Matthew 27.45–56
Saturday	**23 October**	2 Samuel 7.18–end	Acts 2.22–33

Monday	**25 October**	Isaiah 42.14–21	Luke 1.5–25
Tuesday	**26 October**	I Samuel 4.12–end	Luke 1.57–80
Wednesday	**27 October**	Baruch 5 *or* Haggai 1.1–11	Mark 1.1–11
		or 1st EP of Simon and Jude, Apostles	
Thursday	**28 October**	Simon and Jude, Apostles – see p.67	
Friday	**29 October**	2 Samuel 11.1–17	Matthew 14.1–12
Saturday	**30 October**	Isaiah 43.15–21	Acts 19.1–10
		or 1st EP of **All Saints' Day**, *if All Saints' Day is celebrated on*	
		31 October	

Monday	**1 November**	**All Saints' Day** – see p.68	
		or, if All Saints' Day is celebrated on 31 October	
		only, the following readings are used:	
		Esther 3.1–11, 4.7–17	Matthew 18.1–10
Tuesday	**2 November**	Ezekiel 18.21–end	Matthew 18.12–20
Wednesday	**3 November**	Proverbs 3.27–end	Matthew 18.21–end
Thursday	**4 November**	Exodus 23.1–9	Matthew 19.1–15
Friday	**5 November**	Proverbs 3.13–18	Matthew 19.16–end
Saturday	**6 November**	Deuteronomy 28.1–6	Matthew 20.1–16

Monday	**8 November**	Isaiah 40.21–end	Romans 11.25–end
Tuesday	**9 November**	Ezekiel 34.20–end	John 10.1–18
Wednesday	**10 November**	Leviticus 26.3–13	Titus 2.1–10
Thursday	**11 November**	Hosea 6.1–6	Matthew 9.9–13
Friday	**12 November**	Malachi 4	John 4.5–26
Saturday	**13 November**	Micah 6.6–8	Colossians 3.12–17

Monday	**15 November**	Micah 7.1–7	Matthew 10.24–39
Tuesday	**16 November**	Habakkuk 3.1–19a	I Corinthians 4.9–16
Wednesday	**17 November**	Zechariah 8.1–13	Mark 13.3–8
Thursday	**18 November**	Zechariah 10.6–end	I Peter 5.1–11
Friday	**19 November**	Micah 4.1–5	Luke 9.28–36
Saturday	**20 November**	At Evening Prayer the readings for the Eve of Christ the King are used.	
		At other services, the following readings are used:	
		Exodus 16.1–21	John 6.3–15

Monday	**22 November**	Jeremiah 30.1–3, 10–17	Romans 12.9–21
Tuesday	**23 November**	Jeremiah 30.18–24	John 10.22–30
Wednesday	**24 November**	Jeremiah 31.1–9	Matthew 15.21–31
Thursday	**25 November**	Jeremiah 31.10–17	Matthew 16.13–end
Friday	**26 November**	Jeremiah 31.31–37	Hebrews 10.11–18
Saturday	**27 November**	Isaiah 51.17—52.2	Ephesians 5.1–20

¶ Collects and Post Communions

All the contemporary language Collects and Post Communions, including the Additional Collects, may be found in *Common Worship: Collects and Post Communions* (Church House Publishing: London, 2004). The Additional Collects are also published separately.

The contemporary language Collects and Post Communions all appear in *Times and Seasons: President's Edition for Holy Communion*. Apart from the Additional Collects, they appear in the other Common Worship volumes as follows:

¶ President's edition: all Collects and Post Communions;
¶ *Daily Prayer*: all Collects;
¶ main volume: Collects and Post Communions for Sundays, Principal Feasts and Holy Days, and Festivals;
¶ *Festivals*: Collects and Post Communions for Festivals, Lesser Festivals, Common of the Saints and Special Occasions.

The traditional-language Collects and Post Communions all appear in the president's edition. They appear in other publications as follows:

¶ main volume: Collects and Post Communions for Sundays, Principal Feasts and Holy Days, and Festivals;
¶ separate booklet: Collects and Post Communions for Lesser Festivals, Common of the Saints and Special Occasions.

¶ Lectionary for Dedication Festival

If date not known, observe on the first Sunday in October or Last Sunday after Trinity.

Evening Prayer on the Eve
Psalm 24
2 Chronicles 7.11–16
John 4.19–29

Dedication Festival
Gold or White

	Principal Service	3rd Service	2nd Service	Psalmody
Year A	1 Kings 8.22–30 *or* Revelation 21.9–14 Psalm 122 Hebrews 12.18–24 Matthew 21.12–16	Haggai 2.6–9 Hebrews 10.19–25	Jeremiah 7.1–11 1 Corinthians 3.9–17 *HC* Luke 19.1–10	*MP* 48, 150 *EP* 132
Year B	Genesis 28.11–18 *or* Revelation 21.9–14 Psalm 122 1 Peter 2.1–10 John 10.22–29	Haggai 2.6–9 Hebrews 10.19–25	Jeremiah 7.1–11 Luke 19.1–10	*MP* 48, 150 *EP* 132
Year C	1 Chronicles 29.6–19 Psalm 122 Ephesians 2.19–22 John 2.13–22	Haggai 2.6–9 Hebrews 10.19–25	Jeremiah 7.1–11 Luke 19.1–10	*MP* 48, 150 *EP* 132

The Blessed Virgin Mary

Genesis 3.8–15, 20; Isaiah 7.10–14; Micah 5.1–4
Psalms 45.10–17; 113; 131
Acts 1.12–14; Romans 8.18–30; Galatians 4.4–7
Luke 1.26–38; *or* 1.39–47; John 19.25–27

Martyrs

2 Chronicles 24.17–21; Isaiah 43.1–7; Jeremiah 11.18–20; Wisdom 4.10–15
Psalms 3; 11; 31.1–5; 44.18–24; 126
Romans 8.35–end; 2 Corinthians 4.7–15; 2 Timothy 2.3–7 [8–13]; Hebrews 11.32–end;
     1 Peter 4.12–end; Revelation 12.10–12*a*
Matthew 10.16–22; *or* 10.28–39; *or* 16.24–26; John 12.24–26; *or* 15.18–21

Agnes (21 Jan): *also* Revelation 7.13–end
Alban (22 June): *especially* 2 Timothy 2.3–13; John 12.24–26
Alphege (19 Apr): *also* Hebrews 5.1–4
Boniface (5 June): *also* Acts 20.24–28
Charles (30 Jan): *also* Ecclesiasticus 2.12–end; 1 Timothy 6.12–16
Clement (23 Nov): *also* Philippians 3.17—4.3; Matthew 16.13–19
Cyprian (15 Sept): *especially* 1 Peter 4.12–end; *also* Matthew 18.18–22
Edmund (20 Nov): *also* Proverbs 20.28; 21.1–4, 7
Ignatius (17 Oct): *also* Philippians 3.7–12; John 6.52–58
James Hannington (29 Oct): *especially* Matthew 10.28–39
Janani Luwum (17 Feb): *also* Ecclesiasticus 4.20–28; John 12.24–32
John Coleridge Patteson (20 Sept): *especially* 2 Chronicles 24.17–21; *also* Acts 7.55–end
Justin (1 June): *especially* John 15.18–21; *also* 1 Maccabees 2.15–22; 1 Corinthians 1.18–25
Laurence (10 Aug): *also* 2 Corinthians 9.6–10
Lucy (13 Dec): *also* Wisdom 3.1–7; 2 Corinthians 4.6–15
Oswald (5 Aug): *especially* 1 Peter 4.12–end; John 16.29–end
Perpetua, Felicity and comps (7 Mar): *especially* Revelation 12.10–12*a*; *also* Wisdom 3.1–7
Polycarp (23 Feb): *also* Revelation 2.8–11
Thomas Becket (29 Dec *or* 7 Jul): *especially* Matthew 10.28–33; *also* Ecclesiasticus 51.1–8
William Tyndale (6 Oct): *also* Proverbs 8.4–11; 2 Timothy 3.12–end

Teachers of the Faith and Spiritual Writers

I Kings 3.[6–10] 11–14; Proverbs 4.1–9; Wisdom 7.7–10, 15–16; Ecclesiasticus 39.1–10
Psalms 19.7–10; 34.11–17; 37.31–35; 119.89–96; 119.97–104
I Corinthians 1.18–25; *or* 2.1–10; *or* 2.9–end; Ephesians 3.8–12; 2 Timothy 4.1–8;
    Titus 2.1–8
Matthew 5.13–19; *or* 13.52–end; *or* 23.8–12; Mark 4.1–9; John 16.12–15

Ambrose (7 Dec): *also* Isaiah 41.9*b*–13; Luke 22.24–30
Anselm (21 Apr): *also* Wisdom 9.13–end; Romans 5.8–11
Athanasius (2 May): *also* Ecclesiasticus 4.20–28; *also* Matthew 10.24–27
Augustine of Hippo (28 Aug): *especially* Ecclesiasticus 39.1–10; *also* Romans 13.11–13
Basil and Gregory (2 Jan): *especially* 2 Timothy 4.1–8; Matthew 5.13–19
Bernard (20 Aug): *especially* Revelation 19.5–9
Catherine of Siena (29 Apr): *also* Proverbs 8.1, 6–11; John 17.12–end
Francis de Sales (24 Jan): *also* Proverbs 3.13–18; John 3.17–21
Gregory the Great (3 Sept): *also* 1 Thessalonians 2.3–8
Gregory of Nyssa and Macrina (19 July): *especially* 1 Corinthians 2.9–13;
    also Wisdom 9.13–17
Hilary (13 Jan): *also* 1 John 2.18–25; John 8.25–32
Irenaeus (28 June): *also* 2 Peter 1.16–end
Jeremy Taylor (13 Aug); *also* Titus 2.7–8, 11–14
John Bunyan (30 Aug): *also* Hebrews 12.1–2; Luke 21.21, 34–36
John Chrysostom (13 Sept): *especially* Matthew 5.13–19; *also* Jeremiah 1.4–10
John of the Cross (14 Dec): *especially* 1 Corinthians 2.1–10; *also* John 14.18–23
Leo (10 Nov): *also* 1 Peter 5.1–11
Richard Hooker (3 Nov): *especially* John 16.12–15; *also* Ecclesiasticus 44.10–15
Teresa of Avila (15 Oct): *also* Romans 8.22–27
Thomas Aquinas (28 Jan): *especially* Wisdom 7.7–10, 15–16; 1 Corinthians 2.9–end;
    John 16.12–15
William Law (10 Apr): *especially* 1 Corinthians 2.9–end; *also* Matthew 17.1–9

Bishops and Other Pastors

I Samuel 16.1, 6–13; Isaiah 6.1–8; Jeremiah 1.4–10; Ezekiel 3.16–21; Malachi 2.5–7
Psalms 1; 15; 16.5–end; 96; 110
Acts 20.28–35; I Corinthians 4.1–5; 2 Corinthians 4.1–10 [or 1–2, 5–7];
    or 5.14–20; I Peter 5.1–4
Matthew 11.25–end; or 24.42–46; John 10.11–16; or 15.9–17; or 21.15–17

Augustine of Canterbury (26 May): *also* I Thessalonians 2.2b–8; Matthew 13.31–33
Charles Simeon (13 Nov): *especially* Malachi 2.5–7; *also* Colossians 1.3–8; Luke 8.4–8
David (1 Mar): *also* 2 Samuel 23.1–4; Psalm 89.19–22, 24
Dunstan (19 May): *especially* Matthew 24.42–46; *also* Exodus 31.1–5
Edward King (8 Mar): *also* Hebrews 13.1–8
George Herbert (27 Feb): *especially* Malachi 2.5–7; Matthew 11.25–end;
    also Revelation 19.5–9
Hugh (17 Nov); *also* I Timothy 6.11–16
John Keble (14 July): *also* Lamentations 3.19–26; Matthew 5.1–8
John and Charles Wesley (24 May): *also* Ephesians 5.15–20
Lancelot Andrewes (25 Sept): *especially* Isaiah 6.1–8
Martin of Tours (11 Nov): *also* I Thessalonians 5.1–11; Matthew 25.34–40
Nicholas (6 Dec): *also* Isaiah 61.1–3; I Timothy 6.6–11; Mark 10.13–16
Richard (16 June): *also* John 21.15–19
Swithun (15 July): *also* James 5.7–11, 13–18
Thomas Ken (8 June): *especially* 2 Corinthians 4.1–10 [or 1–2, 5–7]; Matthew 24.42–46
Wulfstan (19 Jan): *especially* Matthew 24.42–46

Members of Religious Communities

I Kings 19.9–18; Proverbs 10.27–end; Song of Solomon 8.6–7; Isaiah 61.10—62.5;
    Hosea 2.14–15, 19–20
Psalms 34.1–8; 112.1–9; 119.57–64; 123; 131
Acts 4.32–35; 2 Corinthians 10.17—11.2; Philippians 3.7–14; I John 2.15–17;
    Revelation 19.1, 5–9
Matthew 11.25–end; *or* 19.3–12; *or* 19.23–end; Luke 9.57–end; *or* 12.32–37

Aelred (12 Jan): *also* Ecclesiasticus 15.1–6
Alcuin (20 May): *also* Colossians 3.12–16; John 4.19–24
Antony (17 Jan): *especially* Philippians 3.7–14, *also* Matthew 19.16–26
Bede (25 May): *also* Ecclesiasticus 39.1–10
Benedict (11 July): *also* I Corinthians 3.10–11; Luke 18.18–22
Clare (11 Aug): *especially* Song of Solomon 8.6–7
Dominic (8 Aug): *also* Ecclesiasticus 39.1–10
Etheldreda (23 June): *also* Matthew 25.1–13
Francis of Assisi (4 Oct): *also* Galatians 6.14–end; Luke 12.22–34
Hilda (19 Nov): *especially* Isaiah 61.10—62.5
Hildegard (17 Sept): *also* I Corinthians 2.9–13; Luke 10.21–24
Julian of Norwich (8 May): *also* I Corinthians 13.8–end; Matthew 5.13–16
Vincent de Paul (27 Sept): *also* I Corinthians 1.25–end; Matthew 25.34–40

Missionaries

Isaiah 52.7–10; *or* 61.1–3*a*; Ezekiel 34.11–16; Jonah 3.1–5
Psalms 67; *or* 87; *or* 97; *or* 100; *or* 117
Acts 2.14, 22–36; *or* 13.46–49; *or* 16.6–10; *or* 26.19–23; Romans 15.17–21;
    2 Corinthians 5.11—6.2
Matthew 9.35–end; *or* 28.16–end; Mark 16.15–20; Luke 5.1–11; *or* 10.1–9

Aidan (31 Aug): *also* I Corinthians 9.16–19
Anskar (3 Feb): *especially* Isaiah 52.7–10; *also* Romans 10.11–15
Chad (2 Mar *or* 26 Oct): *also* I Timothy 6.11*b*–16
Columba (9 June): *also* Titus 2.11–end
Cuthbert (20 Mar *or* 4 Sept): *especially* Ezekiel 34.11–16; *also* Matthew 18.12–14
Cyril and Methodius (14 Feb): *especially* Isaiah 52.7–10; *also* Romans 10.11–15
Henry Martyn (19 Oct): *especially* Mark 16.15–end; *also* Isaiah 55.6–11
Ninian (16 Sept): *especially* Acts 13.46–49; Mark 16.15–end
Patrick (17 Mar): *also* Psalm 91.1–4, 13–end; Luke 10.1–12, 17–20
Paulinus (10 Oct); *especially* Matthew 28.16–end
Wilfrid (12 Oct): *especially* Luke 5.1–11; *also* I Corinthians 1.18–25
Willibrord (7 Nov): *especially* Isaiah 52.7–10; Matthew 28.16–end

Any Saint

General

Genesis 12.1–4; Proverbs 8.1–11; Micah 6.6–8; Ecclesiasticus 2.7–13 [14–end]
Psalms 32; 33.1–5; 119.1–8; 139.1–4 [5–12]; 145.8–14
Ephesians 3.14–19; or 6.11–18; Hebrews 13.7–8, 15–16; James 2.14–17;
    1 John 4.7–16; Revelation 21.[1–4] 5–7
Matthew 19.16–21; or 25.1–13; or 25.14–30; John 15.1–8; or 17.20–end

Christian rulers

1 Samuel 16.1–13a; 1 Kings 3.3–14
Psalms 72.1–7; 99
1 Timothy 2.1–6
Mark 10.42–45; Luke 14.27–33

Alfred the Great (26 Oct): *also* 2 Samuel 23.1–5; John 18.33–37
Edward the Confessor (13 Oct): *also* 2 Samuel 23.1–5; 1 John 4.13–16
Margaret of Scotland (16 Nov): *also* Proverbs 31.10–12, 20, 26–end;
    1 Corinthians 12.13—13.3; Matthew 25.34–end

Those working for the poor and underprivileged

Isaiah 58.6–11
Psalms 82; 146.5–10
Hebrews 13.1–3; 1 John 3.14–18
Matthew 5.1–12; or 25.31–end

Elizabeth of Hungary (18 Nov): *especially* Matthew 25.31–end; *also* Proverbs 31.10–end
Josephine Butler (30 May): *especially* Isaiah 58.6–11; *also* 1 John 3.18–23; Matthew 9.10–13
William Wilberforce, Olaudah Equiano and Thomas Clarkson (30 July): *also* Job 31.16–23;
    Galatians 3.26–end, 4.6–7; Luke 4.16–21

Men and women of learning

Proverbs 8.22–31; Ecclesiasticus 44.1–15
Psalms 36.5–10; 49.1–4
Philippians 4.7–8
Matthew 13.44–46, 52; John 7.14–18

Those whose holiness was revealed in marriage and family life

Proverbs 31.10–13, 19–20, 30–end; Tobit 8.4–7
Psalms 127; 128
1 Peter 3.1–9
Mark 3.31–end; Luke 10.38–end

Mary Sumner (9 Aug): *also* Hebrews 13.1–5
Monica (27 Aug): *also* Ecclesiasticus 26.1–3, 13–16

The Guidance of the Holy Spirit

Proverbs 24.3–7; Isaiah 30.15–21; Wisdom 9.13–17
Psalms 25.1–9; 104.26–33; 143.8–10
Acts 15.23–29; Romans 8:22–27; 1 Corinthians 12.4–13
Luke 14.27–33; John 14.23–26; *or* 16.13–15

Rogation Days
(10–12 May in 2021)

Deuteronomy 8.1–10; 1 Kings 8.35–40; Job 28.1–11
Psalms 104.21–30; 107.1–9; 121
Philippians 4.4–7; 2 Thessalonians 3.6–13; 1 John 5.12–15
Matthew 6.1–15; Mark 11.22–24; Luke 11.5–13

Harvest Thanksgiving

Year A	Year B	Year C
Deuteronomy 8.7–18 *or* 28.1–14	Joel 2.21–27	Deuteronomy 26.1–11
Psalm 65	Psalm 126	Psalm 100
2 Corinthians 9.6–end	1 Timothy 2.1–7; *or* 6.6–10	Philippians 4.4–9
Luke 12.16–30; *or* 17.11–19	Matthew 6.25–33	*or* Revelation 14.14–18
		John 6.25–35

Mission and Evangelism

Isaiah 49.1–6; *or* 52.7–10; Micah 4.1–5
Psalms 2; 46; 67
Acts 17.10–end; 2 Corinthians 5.14—6.2; Ephesians 2.13–end
Matthew 5.13–16; *or* 28.16–end; John 17.20–end

The Unity of the Church

Jeremiah 33.6–9*a*; Ezekiel 36.23–28; Zephaniah 3.16–end
Psalms 100; 122; 133
Ephesians 4.1–6; Colossians 3.9–17; 1 John 4.9–15
Matthew 18.19–22; John 11.45–52; *or* 17.11*b*–23

The Peace of the World

Isaiah 9.1–6; *or* 57.15–19; Micah 4.1–5
Psalms 40.14–17; 72.1–7; 85.8–13
Philippians 4.6–9; 1 Timothy 2.1–6; James 3.13–18
Matthew 5.43–end; John 14.23–29; *or* 15.9–17

Social Justice and Responsibility

Isaiah 32.15–end; Amos 5.21–24; *or* 8.4–7; Acts 5.1–11
Psalms 31.21–24; 85.1–7; 146.5–10
Colossians 3.12–15; James 2.1–4
Matthew 5.1–12; *or* 25.31–end; Luke 16.19–end

Ministry, including Ember Days
(See page 7)

Numbers 11.16–17, 24–29; *or* 27.15–end; 1 Samuel 16.1–13*a*; Isaiah 6.1–8;
    or 61.1–3; Jeremiah 1.4–10
Psalms 40.8–13; 84.8–12; 89.19–25; 101.1–5, 7; 122
Acts 20.28–35; 1 Corinthians 3.3–11; Ephesians 4.4–16; Philippians 3.7–14
Luke 4.16–21; *or* 12.35–43; *or* 22.24–27; John 4.31–38; *or* 15.5–17

In Time of Trouble

Genesis 9.8–17; Job 1.13–end; Isaiah 38.6–11
Psalms 86.1–7; 107.4–15; 142.1–7
Romans 3.21–26; Romans 8.18–25; 2 Corinthians 8.1–5, 9
Mark 4.35–end; Luke 12.1–7; John 16.31–end

For the Sovereign

Joshua 1.1–9; Proverbs 8.1–16
Psalms 20; 101; 121
Romans 13.1–10; Revelation 21.22—22.4
Matthew 22.16–22; Luke 22.24–30

The anniversary of HM The Queen's accession is 6 February.

¶ *Psalms in the Course of a Month*

The following provision may be used for a monthly cycle of psalmody in place of the psalms provided in the tables in this booklet. It is based on the provision in The Book of Common Prayer.

	Morning Prayer	**Evening Prayer**
1	1—5	6—8
2	9—11	12—14
3	15—17	18
4	19—21	22—23
5	24—26	27—29
6	30—31	32—34
7	35—36	37
8	38—40	41—43
9	44—46	47—49
10	50—52	53—55
11	56—58	59—61
12	62—64	65—67
13	68	69—70
14	71—72	73—74
15	75—77	78
16	79—81	82—85
17	86—88	89
18	90—92	93—94
19	95—97	98—101
20	102—103	104
21	105	106
22	107	108—109
23	110—112	113—115
24	116—118	119.1–32
25	119.33–72	119.73–96
26	119.97–144	119.145–176
27	120—125	126—131
28	132—135	136—138
29	139—140	141—143
30	144—146	147—150

In February the psalms are read only to the 28th or 29th day of the month.

In January, March, May, July, August, October and December, all of which have 31 days, the same psalms are read on the last day of the month (being an ordinary weekday) which were read the day before, or else the psalms of the monthly course omitted on one of the Sundays in that month.

Concise Calendar November 2021 – December 2022

Advent 2021 to the eve of Advent 2022: Year C (Daily Eucharistic Lectionary Year 2)

	November 2021					December 2021					January 2022				
Sunday		3bAdv	2bAdv	ChrK	AdvI		Adv2	Adv3	Adv4	ChrI		Chr2	Bapt	Ep2	Ep3	Ep4
Monday	AllSs	8	15	22	29		6	13	20	27		3	10	17	24	31
Tuesday	2	9	16	23	30		7	14	21	28		4	11	18	25	
Wednesday	3	10	17	24		1	8	15	22	29		5	12	19	26	
Thursday	4	11	18	25		2	9	16	23	30		Epiph	13	20	27	
Friday	5	12	19	26		3	10	17	24	31		7	14	21	28	
Saturday	6	13	20	27		4	11	18	Chr		1	8	15	22	29	

	February 2022					March 2022					April 2022				
Sunday		4bLn	3bLn	2bLnt	NbLnt		LntI	Lnt2	Lnt3	Lnt4		Lnt5	PmS	Est	Est2
Monday		7	14	21	28		7	14	21	28		4	11	18	25
Tuesday	1	8	15	22		1	8	15	22	29		5	12	19	26
Wednesday	Pres	9	16	23		Ash W	9	16	23	30		6	13	20	27
Thursday	3	10	17	24		3	10	17	24	31		7	14	21	28
Friday	4	11	18	25		4	11	18	Ann		1	8	15	22	29
Saturday	5	12	19	26		5	12	19	27		2	9	16	23	30

	May 2022					June 2022					July 2022				
Sunday	Est3	Est4	Est5	Est6	Est7		Pent	TrS	TrI	Tr2		Tr3	Tr4	Tr5	Tr6	Tr7
Monday	2	9	16	23	30		6	13	20	27		4	11	18	25
Tuesday	3	10	17	24	31		7	14	21	28		5	12	19	26
Wednesday	4	11	18	25		1	8	15	22	29		6	13	20	27
Thursday	5	12	19	Ascn		2	9	16	23	30		7	14	21	28
Friday	6	13	20	27		3	10	17	24		1	8	15	22	29
Saturday	7	14	21	28		4	11	18	25		2	9	16	23	30

	August 2022					September 2022					October 2022				
Sunday		Tr8	Tr9	Tr10	Tr11		Tr12	Tr13	Tr14	Tr15		Tr16	Tr17	Tr118	LstTr	4bAdv
Monday	1	8	15	22	29		5	12	19	26		3	10	17	24	31
Tuesday	2	9	16	23	30		6	13	20	27		4	11	18	25
Wednesday	3	10	17	24	31		7	14	21	28		5	12	19	26
Thursday	4	11	18	25		1	8	15	22	29		6	13	20	27
Friday	5	12	19	26		2	9	16	23	30		7	14	21	28
Saturday	6	13	20	27		3	10	17	24		1	8	15	22	29

	November 2022					December 2022				
Sunday		3bAdv	2bAdv	ChrK	AdvI		Adv2	Adv3	Adv4	Chr
Monday		7	14	21	28		5	12	19	26
Tuesday	AllSs	8	15	22	29		6	13	20	27
Wednesday	2	9	16	23	30		7	14	21	28
Thursday	3	10	17	24		1	8	15	22	29
Friday	4	11	18	25		2	9	16	23	30
Saturday	5	12	19	26		3	10	17	24	31

On Sunday 26 December 2021 Stephen, deacon, first martyr may be celebrated.

On Sunday 2 January **The Epiphany** may be celebrated, transferred from 6 January.

On Sunday 30 January **The Presentation of Christ** may be celebrated, transferred from 2 February.

On Sunday 30 October **All Saints' Day** may be celebrated, transferred from 1 November.

REFLECTIONS FOR SUNDAYS (YEAR B)

Reflections for Sundays offers over 250 reflections on the Principal Readings for every Sunday and major Holy Day in Year B, from the same experienced team of writers that have made *Reflections for Daily Prayer* so successful. For each Sunday and major Holy Day, they provide:

- full lectionary details for the Principal Service
- a reflection on each Old Testament reading (both Continuous and Related)
- a reflection on the Epistle
- a reflection on the Gospel.

This book also contains a substantial introduction to the Gospel of Matthew, written by Paula Gooder.

£14.99 • 288 pages
ISBN 978 1 78140 030 2

REFLECTIONS ON THE PSALMS

Reflections on the Psalms provides original and insightful meditations on each of the Bible's 150 Psalms.

Each reflection is accompanied by its corresponding Psalm refrain and prayer from the *Common Worship Psalter*, making this a valuable resource for personal or devotional use.

Specially written introductions by Paula Gooder and Steven Croft explore the Psalms and the Bible and the Psalms in the life of the Church.

£14.99 • 192 pages
ISBN 978 0 7151 4490 9

REFLECTIONS FOR DAILY PRAYER 2020/21

Enhance your spiritual journey through the rich landscape of the Church's year with *Reflections for Daily Prayer*, the Church of England's daily prayer companion. Covering Monday to Saturday each week from Advent 2020 to Eve of Advent 2021, *Reflections for Daily Prayer* offers stimulating reflections on a Bible reading from the lectionary for *Common Worship: Morning Prayer*. Thousands of readers value the creative insights, scholarship and pastoral wisdom offered by our team of experienced writers.

Each day includes:

- full lectionary details for Morning Prayer
- a reflection on one of the Bible readings
- a Collect for the day.

£16.99 • 336 pages
ISBN 978 1 78140 179 8

Also available in Kindle and epub formats, and as an app

This book also contains:

- a simple form of Morning Prayer, with seasonal variations, for use throughout the year
- a short form of Night Prayer (also known as Compline)
- a guide to the practice of daily prayer by Rachel Treweek.

COMMON WORSHIP: DAILY PRAYER

The official daily office of the Church of England, **Common Worship: Daily Prayer** is a rich collection of devotional material that will enable those wanting to enrich their quiet times to develop a regular pattern of prayer. It includes:

- Prayer During the Day
- Forms of Penitence
- Morning and Evening Prayer
- Night Prayer (Compline)
- Collects and Refrains
- Canticles
- Complete Psalter

896 pages • with 6 ribbons • 202 x 125mm

Hardback	978 0 7151 2199 3	**£22.50**
Soft cased	978 0 7151 2178 8	**£27.50**
Bonded leather	978 0 7151 2277 8	**£50.00**